Visual Science Encyclopedia

Rocks Minerals and Soil

▲ This deep red soil profile is typical of soils that form in the tropics. High temperature weathering makes iron oxides turn red, unlike in cooler parts of the world, where the oxides are brown.

How to use this book

Every word defined in this book can be found in alphabetical order on pages 3 to 47. There is also a full index on page 48. A number of other features will help you get the most out of the *Visual Science Encyclopedia*. They are shown below.

Here you will find the first word defined on any left-hand page.

Here you will find the last word defined on any right-hand page.

Each word is shown in bold so it is easy to find.

Each new letter of the alphabet is clearly marked to help you find the word you are looking for quicker.

Other words defined in the book are highlighted in bold.

Plus, many entries point to related words of interest.

Illustrations for some words complement the text and provide further information on a topic.

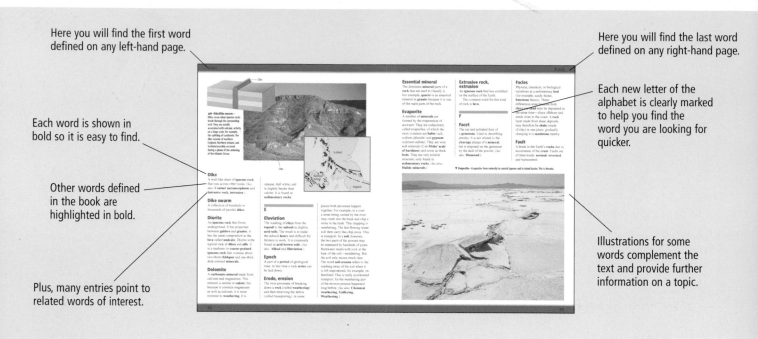

Acknowledgments

Grolier Educational
First published in the United States in 2002 by Grolier Educational, Sherman Turnpike, Danbury, CT 06816

Copyright © 2002
Atlantic Europe Publishing Company Ltd.

Author
Brian Knapp, BSc, PhD

Art Director
Duncan McCrae, BSc

Senior Designer
Adele Humphries, BA, PGCE

Editors
Lisa Magloff, BA, and Mary Sanders, BSc

Illustrations
David Woodroffe

Designed and produced by
EARTHSCAPE EDITIONS

Reproduced in Malaysia by
Global Color

Printed in Hong Kong by
Wing King Tong Company Ltd.

Library of Congress Cataloging-in-Publication Data
Visual Science Encyclopedia
      p. cm.
   Includes indexes.
   Contents: v. 1. Weather—v. 2. Elements—v. 3. Rocks, minerals, and soil—v. 4. Forces—v. 5. Light and sound—v. 6. Water—v. 7. Plants—v. 8. Electricity and magnetism—v. 9. Earth and space—v. 10. Computers and the Internet—v. 11. Earthquakes and volcanoes—v. 12. Heat and energy.
   ISBN 0-7172-5595-6 (set: alk. paper)—ISBN 0-7172-5596-4 (v. 1: alk. paper)—ISBN 0-7172-5597-2 (v. 2: alk. paper)—ISBN 0-7172-5598-0 (v. 3: alk. paper)—ISBN 0-7172-5599-9 (v. 4: alk. paper)—ISBN 0-7172-5600-6 (v. 5: alk. paper)—ISBN 0-7172-5601-4 (v. 6: alk. paper)—ISBN 0-7172-5602-2 (v. 7: alk. paper)—ISBN 0-7172-5603-0 (v. 8: alk. paper)—ISBN 0-7172-5604-9 (v. 9: alk. paper)—ISBN 0-7172-5605-7 (v. 10: alk. paper)—ISBN 0-7172-5606-5 (v. 11: alk. paper)—ISBN 0-7172-5607-3 (v. 12: alk. paper)
   1. Science—Encyclopedias, Juvenile. [1. Science—Encyclopedias.] I. Grolier Educational (Firm)
   QI21.V58 2001
   503—dc21
                              2001023704

Picture credits
All photographs are from the Earthscape Editions photolibrary except the following:
(c=center t=top b=bottom l=left r=right)
The British Coal Corporation 13tr.

This product is manufactured from sustainable managed forests. For every tree cut down, at least one more is planted.

A

Abrasion

The rubbing away (**erosion**) of a **rock** due to the scraping of **sand** or large material carried by water, wind, or ice.

Acid brown soil

A **brown soil** that has a **pH** of about 5. In this kind of **soil** there is not enough **humus** to bind all of the **topsoil** together, and the **clays** are washed down into the **subsoil**, making it **heavy** and **waterlogged**. (*See also:* **Eluviation** and **Illuviation**.)

Acid rock

A type of **igneous rock** that consists predominantly of light-colored **minerals** and more than two-thirds **silica** (for example, **granite**).

Acid soil

A **soil** with a **pH** of less than 7. A slightly acid soil (from pH 7 down to pH 5.5) still has enough **nutrients** in it for good plant growth. Most farmland soils in the cool, humid parts of the world (those with **brown soils** or **gray-brown soils**) are slightly acid. However, a strongly acid soil (with a pH below 5.5) has relatively few nutrients in it and so is, in general, an infertile soil. This kind of soil will only support plants that are specially adapted for scavenging nutrients. These plants include heath plants and coniferous trees. Tropical rain-forest trees are also adapted to living on very acid soils.

In general, very acid soils occur for two reasons: The **rock** from which they develop may contain few nutrients (for example a **sandstone** or a **granite**), or the

▼ **Acid brown soil**—A soil that produces a strong acid reaction, and in which clays move downward, causing the pores in the subsoil to be blocked by clay, giving the subsoil a much heavier texture than the topsoil. However, no iron moves, and so the soil is brown throughout. A greater degree of acidity would lead to a podzol soil forming.

rainfall is heavy enough to wash the nutrients away as they are released from the rock by **weathering** (as is the case in moorlands and in tropical rain forests). (*See also:* **Eluviation**; **Leach, leaching**; **Moder**; **Mor**; **Podzol**.)

Agglomerate

A **rock** made from the compacted particles thrown out by a volcano (for example, **tuff**).

▲ **Agglomerate**—An agglomerate with many angular fragments of different sizes fused together.

A horizon

The term used by soil scientists for the upper part of the **soil** that contains a mixture of finely ground **rocks** and **minerals** (such as **sand** and **clay**), and **organic matter** (such as **humus**). It is a more technical way of referring to the **topsoil**.

The A horizon gives a good indication of what is going on in a soil. If the A horizon is a dark red or brown and merges gradually into the **B horizon (subsoil)** below it, then the soil is usually **fertile** and good for crops. If the A horizon contains well-marked layers, and especially if the upper layer is thin and gray in color, then the soil is

acidic and will not support crops.

A deep A horizon is usually best for crop growth. The deepest A horizons occur in soils called **chernozems**. They are the soils of the prairies. The A horizons of chernozems are black and may be a meter or more thick. This is why, with sufficient **irrigation**, they are among the world's most productive soils. (*See also:* **Horizon**.)

Alfisol

A **soil** type found naturally in cool, humid, regions with broad-leaved forests. It is also called a **brown soil** or brown earth.

▼ **A horizon**—The A horizon, or topsoil, can be identified as the part that contains most of the fibrous plant roots as shown by this grass clump. The dark color of the soil indicates that it is fertile.

It is the second most abundant soil in the world, accounting for about 15% of the world soils.

Alfisols have good fertility (*see:* **Fertile soil**) and are rich in **clays**, and so hold **moisture** well. At the same time, they have a large amount of **humus**, and this, combined with the ground-breaking activity of the tree roots, helps keep the soil well aerated and drained.

The clays in these soils are important because their surfaces trap **nutrients** released by **weathering** or carried down from the surface by rainwater passing through rotting humus. They are the soils on which most of the world's barley, corn, and wheat are grown.

Alkaline rock

A type of **igneous rock** containing less than half **silica** and normally dominated by dark-colored **minerals** (for example, **gabbro**).

Alkaline soil

A **soil** with a **pH** of more than 7. Alkaline soils are rich in **nutrients**. There are two reasons for this. First, they may have been formed on very **alkaline rocks** such as **chalk** and **limestone**. Typical alkaline soils of this kind are called **rendzinas**. Alternatively, the nutrients are kept in the soil because the rainfall is too low to wash them away. This is the case in **chestnut soils**, which develop on the less humid prairies and Great Plains of North America. However, if the rainfall is very low, then some harmful substances, such as salt, are not washed out of the soil, and they will keep plants from growing. This occurs in the soils of the dry prairies. (*See also:* **Salinization**.)

Alluvial soil

A **soil** that has formed on materials recently deposited on the floodplain of a river (as alluvium).

It is a very young soil, and there has been little chance for soil **horizons** to form. Most alluvial soils are very **fertile**, not because of the rock on which they are deposited, but because each flood washes **nutrients** carried by the rivers into the alluvium.

The high level of fertility has meant that alluvial soils have been some of the most productive and treasured soils in the world. The Ancient Egyptian civilization was founded on the alluvial soils of the Nile River. For thousands of years the Egyptians continued to rely on the yearly flood and its renewal of nutrients. However, in the last half century, since the building of the Aswan High Dam, the land has not flooded, and the soil has become less fertile. As a result, farmers now have to use expensive **fertilizers** on the soil. (*See also:* **Breccia**.)

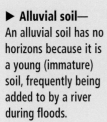

▶ **Alluvial soil—**
An alluvial soil has no horizons because it is a young (immature) soil, frequently being added to by a river during floods.

Amygdule

A **vesicle** in a volcanic **rock** (*see:* **Igneous rock**) filled with secondary **minerals** such as **calcite**, **quartz**, or zeolite.

Andesite

A type of **lava** halfway in properties between **rhyolite** and **basalt**. Andesite is the most common form of lava associated with explosive volcanoes. Its name comes from the active Andean volcanoes.

▶ **Andesite—**Andesite is one of the most common lavas associated with explosive volcanoes.

Andesite makes up the main material of a volcanic cone. Andesitic lava contains many cavities. It may be light colored, but is normally dark, especially brown. Although it is not a particularly acid lava, it is still reasonably sticky and so forms short lava flows that usually develop into tongues that move short distances down the sides of composite volcanoes. (*See also:* **Diorite**.)

Anthracite

A type of **coal** containing almost pure carbon.

Aquiclude

A **rock** that will not let water flow through it. An aquiclude is an **impermeable** rock. It can be a **cap rock**, preventing, for example, the escape of oil from rocks below it, or it can be below an **aquifer**, preventing water from flowing into the ground any further and forcing it to move to the surface as a spring. If an aquifer is sandwiched between two aquicludes, the water in the aquifer is trapped and under pressure.

Aquifer

A **rock** that has a network of connecting spaces that will allow water to seep through it. An aquifer is made of a **permeable** rock. Common aquifers are **limestone**, **chalk**, and **sandstone**. Springs occur where the saturated part of the aquifer reaches the surface. Water does not seep from an aquifer if the rocks below are watertight (**aquicludes**).

Arenaceous

A **rock** composed largely of **sand grains**. **Sandstone** is an arenaceous rock.

▼ **Arenaceous**—Detail of a sandstone, showing the sand grains.

▶ **Argillaceous**—Detail of a shale, showing the fineness of the grains and the way it breaks into sheets.

Argillaceous

A **rock** composed largely of **clay**. **Shale** is an argillaceous rock.

Arkose

A **sandstone rock** made from coarse **grains**. It is produced by the disintegration of a **granite**.

Ash

Fine powdery material thrown out of a volcano. (*See also:* **Igneous rock** and **Tuff**.)

Augite

A dark green **silicate mineral** containing calcium, sodium, iron, aluminum, and magnesium. (*See also:* **Ferromagnesium mineral**.)

Axis of symmetry

A line or plane around which one part of a **crystal** is a mirror image of another part. **Crystal systems** are based on their symmetry.

Augite

◀ **Augite**— Augite is the black crystal in this piece of rock.

Basic rock

An **igneous rock** (for example, **gabbro**, **basalt**) with a high percentage of dark-colored **minerals** and relatively little **silica**.

B

Basalt

A black, basic, **fine-grained**, **igneous** volcanic **rock**. Basaltic **lava** often contains **vesicles**.

Basalt is the most common rock on the Earth's surface, covering all of the world's ocean floors. It is produced at the boundaries of the world's great **tectonic plates** and pours out onto the seabed as the plates pull apart. Hawaii and Iceland are volcanic islands that are made entirely from basalt.

Although basalts are found mainly close to cracks in the ocean floors, they also exist on land, for example, actively in Iceland and Hawaii. Historically, basalt has been pushed out from the mantle to form enormous streams of lava called **flood basalts**, which have solidified into vast black sheets. They are called basalt plateaus or traps. The name trap comes from the world's largest region of flood basalts, the Deccan Traps, India. Large areas of flood basalts also occur in the Columbia-Snake region of the northwestern United States and in the Paraña Basin of South America.

Sierra Nevada
batholith

Batholith

A very large body of **rock** that was intruded deep into the Earth's **crust** and is now exposed by **erosion** (*see:* **Intrusive rock, intrusion**). The rocks found in batholiths are **granites** or granodiorites.

Batholiths can extend for hundreds of square kilometers. The Sierra Nevada Mountains in

▲ **Batholith**—Batholiths make up the backbone of the Sierra Nevada Mountains of California, as shown on this map. The gray speckled rocks help frame the dramatic landscape of Yosemite National Park.

California are made of a string of batholiths. Yosemite National Park in California has magnificent exposures of granodiorite. (*See also:* **Boss**; **Contact metamorphism**; **Igneous rock**; **Metamorphic aureole**; **Stock**.)

Bauxite

The principal **ore** of aluminum. It is a soft, yellow-brown material found close to the surface. It is normally extracted by open-pit mining methods. It is an **oxide** of aluminum.

▲▶ **Basalt**—Basalt is a dark volcanic rock that flows as sheets and forms stepped, or trap, landscapes, as here in the Columbia River basin, Idaho.

Basalt cools to form very distinctive six-sided columns. (*See also:* **Basic rock**; **Dike**; **Gabbro**; **Hornblende**; **Sill**.)

Bed

A layer of **sediment**. It may be produced by a long or a short time during which sand, silt, or clay settles out. The start and end of a bed are marked by a **bedding plane**.

(*See also:* **Chalk; Crossbedding; Current bedding; Facies; Formation; Halite**.)

Bedding plane

An ancient surface marking the meeting point between layers, or **beds**, of **sediment**. **Sedimentary rocks** often split along bedding planes.

B horizon

A word used by **soil** scientists to describe the **subsoil**. The B horizon does not contain **humus**. It is therefore usually a much lighter color than the humus-rich **A horizon**, or **topsoil**.

The B horizon is the place where the taproots of plants are found, while the fine, fibrous, **nutrient**-gathering roots of plants are found in the A horizon close to the surface.

▼ **Bed**—When beds slope, they are called dipping beds. They are clearly seen in this coastal picture.

The B horizon may contain deposits of **minerals** or **clay** washed out of the A horizon. One of the most distinctive of these layers in a B horizon is called an **iron pan**. It is a layer so rich in iron that it forms a brittle sheet that will not let water through. Iron pans of this kind form in **podzol** soils. An even thicker layer of iron occurs in a tropical soil known as a **laterite**. (*See also:* **Horizon**.)

▲ **Biotite**—
Biotite is the black form of mica that is found in many igneous rocks.

Biotite

A black form of the mineral **mica**. Biotite is an important **mineral** in **granite** rocks, showing as the black flecks among the other light-colored minerals.

Black cotton soil

(*See:* **Black soil**.)

Black soil

A term covering two different types of **soil**. It is used for the soils with deep **humus**-rich **topsoils** such as **chernozems**. It is also used for deep soils such as black cotton soils (also called **vertisols**) that develop in subtropical regions over **basalt** and other clay-rich materials. In general, the black color is produced by humus staining, and so all types of black soils are **fertile**.

▶ **Beryl**—Beryl is a green mineral whose crystals have a hexagonal shape.

Beryl

A glassy-green **mineral**. The name beryl comes from the Greek word *beryllos*, meaning a "green gem." It is often found in large pieces, sometimes several meters long.

(*See also:* **Hexagonal**.)

Boss

An upward protrusion of a **batholith**. Some bosses may once have been the **magma** chambers of volcanoes. In England Land's End and Dartmoor are bosses that form apparently quite separate areas of rugged **granite** landscape. However, out of sight below them they are connected by the main batholith.

Botryoidal

The shape of a **mineral** that resembles a bunch of grapes, for example, **hematite**—the **crystals** of which are often arranged in massive clumps, producing a surface covered with spherical bulges.

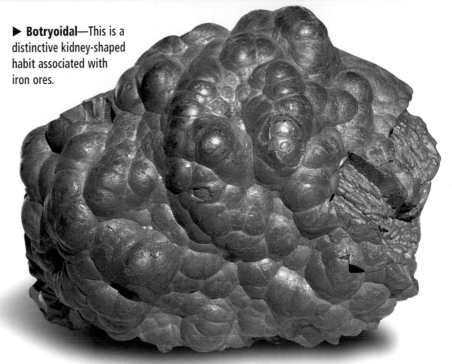

▶ Botryoidal—This is a distinctive kidney-shaped habit associated with iron ores.

Breccia

Large angular fragments of **rock** (rubble) that have been cemented together. The term comes from the Italian for fragments of stone. The rubbly **alluvial** cones at the foot of a mountain front produce angular material of this kind. Broken pieces of **lava** in cinder cones can also become cemented together. This is called volcanic breccia.

In general, the gaps between the stones are filled in with smaller material, often of **sand** size. The fine material and the coarser fragments are then cemented together, often with calcium carbonate that was deposited on the surfaces of the particles as lime-rich water **percolated** naturally through the **sediment** as it formed.

For breccias to keep their sharp edges and corners, they must travel only a short distance. As a result, breccias are found close to the rocks from which they were made. (*See also:* **Coarse-grained rocks**.)

▶ Breccia—A rock made from large pieces of rubble.

Brown soil, brown earth

Moderately dark, brown **soils** found beneath oak and other trees that shed their leaves seasonally. They are part of the soil group called **alfisols**. (*See also:* **Acid soil**.)

Brown soils mainly form on **clay** rocks. Each year the deciduous trees lose their leaves, returning **nutrients** to the soil. As a result of this recycling of nutrients, the **humus** is nearly neutral, and no harmful acids are produced. In turn, this means that the soil is suited to a wide range of animal life, including earthworms. Earthworms pull humus into the soil and turn over the upper levels of the soil, so that there is a good mixing of **organic** and **mineral matter**.

There is no sharp boundary between **A horizon** (**topsoil**) and **B horizon** (**subsoil**), as might be found, for example, in a **podzol** soil. Instead, there is a gradual change, known as a merging horizon.

Brown soils are used for crops and pasture, and form important farmlands in western Europe, the eastern United States, coastal Washington and British Columbia, as well as on South Island of New Zealand.

C

Calcareous rock

A **rock** composed mainly of calcium carbonate (**calcite**).

Calcareous soil

A **soil** containing free calcium (and which is therefore usually **fertile**).

Calcite

The main element in **limestone** and also in many animal shells. It is extracted by living things directly from seawater and then made into shells.

Calcite (calcium **carbonate**) is colorless or white, but often occurs as **grains** rather than **crystals** mixed with other materials, such as **clay**. In this case the rock looks gray.

Calcite is soft (3 on **Mohs' scale of hardness**) and commonly found in **sedimentary rocks**. It is also found in **metamorphic rocks** as **marble**. Calcite is readily dissolved by water. (*See also:* **Gangue**.)

Cap rock

A **rock** that overlies other rocks and protects them in some way. A cap rock can make the lip to a waterfall, the flat top surface of a plateau, or the **impermeable** rock that traps oil or water below it. (*See also:* **Aquiclude**; **Petroleum**; **Reservoir rock**.)

Carbonate minerals

Minerals that contain carbon and oxygen (carbonates, for example, **calcite**, calcium carbonate).

◄▲ **Chalk**—Chalk is a soft, white rock that can make spectacular cliffs. These are near Dover, England.

Central vent volcano

(*See:* **Stratovolcano**.)

Chalk

A soft **limestone rock** made of the skeletons of microscopic sea creatures. Chalks are soft and **permeable rocks**. They form massive **beds** and produce striking landscape features such as England's White Cliffs of Dover (*See also:* **Calcite**.)

Chemical rock

A **rock** produced by chemical precipitation (for example, rock salt, **halite**). Most of these rocks form in the bottoms of lagoons or inland lakes when **mineral**-rich water evaporates, leaving the minerals behind. The salt lakes of Utah and neighboring states have many such deposits, and some of them are mined. In Poland salt deposits are so thick that a cathedral has been carved from salt in one of the mines.

Chemical weathering

The decay, or rotting, of a **rock** through the chemical action of water containing dissolved acidic gases.

Most rainwater has gases dissolved in it. They combine with the water to make it weakly acid. This is the reason chemical weathering is important in all but deserts. The process is normally very slow, except with very reactive rocks such as **limestone**.

Chemical weathering occurs on the surface of a rock, as acidic water reacts with the **minerals**. Some of the substances produced are soluble and are carried away by the rain, while others are insoluble and remain behind. The main insoluble material is called **clay**.

▲ Chemical weathering— Chemical action works from the outside in, producing a kind of onion-skin effect surrounding the remains of the unweathered rock.

▼ Chemical weathering—Take a small piece of chalk, and put it in a glass with some vinegar. The vinegar is an acid, so the chalk will slowly disappear.

▲ Chemical weathering—When a rock has been chemically weathered, it has no strength and breaks up as soon as it is dropped.

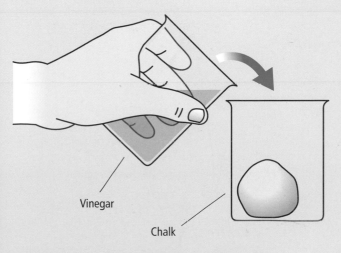

Vinegar

Chalk

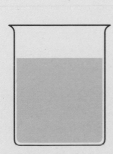

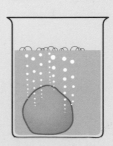

Chernozem

The name for a **soil** group found in the more humid parts of the prairies and Russian steppes. It is also known as a **black soil**.

The soil has a black **A horizon** (**topsoil**) that is at least 25cm thick, and often as much as 1m. The blackness of this layer comes from the **humus** in it.

Chernozems form in places with cold winters and dry summers. Plants that grow in these places have to survive difficult weather conditions of summer drought and fire, and winter freezing. To protect their delicate growing buds, most plants keep about nine-tenths of their bulk under the surface.

The prairies and steppes are dominated by grasses with very extensive fibrous root systems that penetrate downward in a search for **moisture**. When the roots die, they are turned into humus. Furthermore, because the rainfall is low, the humus is not washed out of the soil.

The deep topsoil in a chernozem merges into the **subsoil** (the **B horizon**). The subsoil is often rich in calcium. These are extremely **fertile soils** and widely used (often with **irrigation**) for growing crops.

Chestnut soil

Similar to **chernozem** soils, but their **topsoil** is shallower and less deeply stained. They develop in the areas between the prairies and the deserts. The topsoil is chestnut rather than black because they develop in areas where there is less rainfall, and so plants grow less vigorously and develop smaller root systems. This means that less **humus** gets into the **soils**. Chestnut soils can be used for cultivation, but only with **irrigation**. They are more fragile than chernozems and prone to erosion by wind or heavy rain. (*See also:* **Alkaline soil**.)

C horizon

The name of the lowest layer in a soil. It is also known as the **parent material** of a soil. It is the layer from which new **topsoil** and **subsoil** will form. It is commonly made of unweathered **rock** or **alluvium**.

Cinder cone

A volcanic cone made entirely of cinders. Cinder cones are not as large as volcanic cones made of **ash**, but they have very steep sides.

Clast

An individual **grain** of a **rock**.

Clastic rock

A **sedimentary rock** that is made up of **clasts** of older rocks. For example, **sandstones** and **clays**.

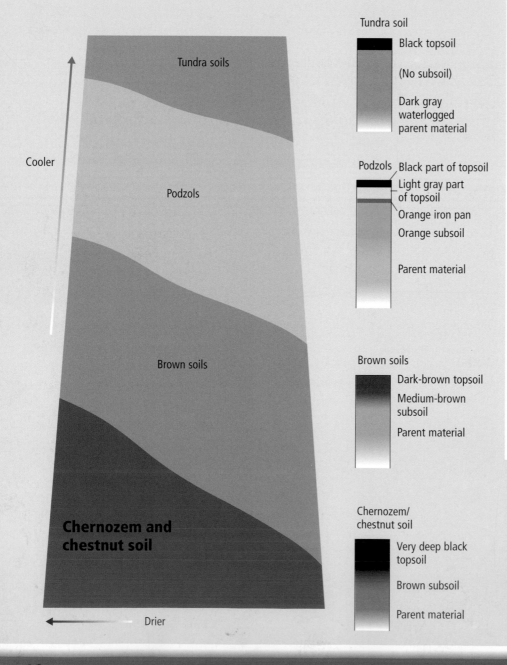

Tundra soil
- Black topsoil
- (No subsoil)
- Dark gray waterlogged parent material

Podzols
- Black part of topsoil
- Light gray part of topsoil
- Orange iron pan
- Orange subsoil
- Parent material

Brown soils
- Dark-brown topsoil
- Medium-brown subsoil
- Parent material

Chernozem/ chestnut soil
- Very deep black topsoil
- Brown subsoil
- Parent material

◄ **Chernozem/Chestnut soil**—These are two related prairie soils. Chernozems are found in the wetter regions, while chestnut soils are found on the more arid edges. Both have thick, black topsoils, but the chernozem is the thickest by far. This map of Saskatchewan shows chestnut soils in warmer and drier parts of the province (to the southwest) than the chernozems. Other soils are found in the cooler and wetter parts of the Province.

Clay

Those rock or soil particles with a diameter of less than 0.005 millimeter. They are the smallest size of **soil** particle. Clay is also the name given to the **mineral** that makes this kind of particle.

Clay particles do not form from the wearing away of larger pieces of **rock**. They are only produced by **chemical weathering**. As chemical weathering goes on, tiny **crystals** of clay are produced, made exclusively of clay minerals. (*See also:* **Feldspar**.)

Clay particles are so small that water cannot easily get between them. That is why clay soils **waterlog** easily. Clay particles also stick together easily. As a result, clay soils are "**heavy**" and are difficult to use for growing crops. They often need special kinds of drainage.

Pure deposits of clay are widely used to make pottery and bricks. (*See also:* **Alfisol**; **Argillaceous**; **Clastic rock**; **Eluviation**; **Flocculation**; **Friable**.)

Clay minerals

Secondary **minerals**, meaning that they do not occur in either igneous or metamorphic rocks, but only as a result of the weathering of minerals in these rocks. Clays are a major constituent of **mudstone** and **shale**. Crystals of clay minerals are so small that they cannot be seen except with the most powerful electron microscope. They are platelike in structure. Weathered **feldspar** is the main source of clay minerals.

Clay soil

A **soil** in which the percentage of **clay** is greater than any other size of material. Clay soils are often hard to work, and they

▶ **Coal**—This is steam coal, a less carbon-rich form of coal than anthracite, but a typical coal of home hearths and power plants.

waterlog easily (they are known as **heavy soils**).

Cleavage

The tendency of some **minerals** to break along one or more lines of weakness. Some **crystals** have well-developed cleavage, as is the case with **mica**. However, in other minerals, such as **quartz**, there is no cleavage. (*See also:* **Fracture**.)

Coal

The carbon-rich, solid **mineral** derived from fossilized plant remains (**fossils**). It is found as bands, called seams, between other kinds of **sedimentary rocks**. Types of coal include bituminous, brown, lignite, and **anthracite**. Coal is also one of the most important fossil **fuels**.

Coal forms when forests grow in swampy conditions. As trees die, they topple into the swamp waters. These waters are acidic and contain little oxygen. As a result,

plants decay only slowly in them. Over thousands of years fallen plant material becomes compressed by the weight of new material falling on old. This process does not, however, directly produce coal. For coal to form, the compressed plant remains have to be buried by many layers of **rock** so that they are changed by heat and pressure. First, the water is squeezed out, together with some of the materials in the wood, leaving only the carbon behind. Then the compressed material becomes hot as chemical changes take place. The degree to which these changes occur is responsible for the different categories of coal. The most complete change results in the type of coal called anthracite. Anthracite contains only carbon and so burns without smoke; other coals have the remains of other materials in them and so produce smoke when they burn. (*See also:* **Cyclothem**.)

Coarse-grained rocks

Rocks made of particles bigger than **sand**. The main rocks are **conglomerates** and **breccias**, which are made of boulders, pebbles, and gravel.

Color, soil

The color of a **soil** layer depends largely on the staining effects of **humus** and iron **oxide**. Humus makes soil black, and iron stains it orange (rust). A dark-brown soil is stained by a mixture of iron oxide and humus. A black soil layer is dominated by humus, and a bright orange soil layer is dominated by iron oxide. A gray layer near the top of a **podzol** soil has neither humus nor iron oxide, both having been **leached** away by strong acids **percolating** down from the soil surface.

Compost

A pile of partly decayed plants. Compost does not occur naturally. Compost is made by heaping waste matter from gardens or farms in such a way as to make conditions very suitable for microorganisms (called decomposers) to break down the plant matter quickly, releasing heat. The crumbly material that results has no signs of the original plants. **Humus** is a word for the material in compost.

Conglomerate

Anything larger than **grit** that has completely rounded particles. Conglomerates can form from pebbly beach materials as well as from river beds.

The main agent for movement is running water. The result is that the particles get sorted, with the coarsest traveling a shorter distance than the finest. The presence of all sizes together suggests a series of short floods, such as would be common in deserts. The presence of particles of much the same size suggests the sorting may have been on a beach. The cementing agent for conglomerates is normally calcium **carbonate**, deposited from the waters that seeped through them. (*See also:* **Coarse-grained rocks**; **Layered rock**; **Sediment**.)

Conservation, soil

The attempt to prevent **soils** from being blown or washed away or from becoming infertile due to overuse. Most attempts at soil conservation try to keep the soil covered with plants to prevent soil erosion. If plants are plowed into the soil, then they can provide the **humus** that tackles infertility and at the same time holds fine soil particles together. The use of calcium also causes clay particles to clump together and resist erosion.

Contact metamorphism

Changes in rock that occur as a result of direct contact with a molten **magma**. Contact metamorphism happens next to **dikes** and **sills**, and more especially close to **batholiths**. In this zone of change the enormous heat causes the rocks to alter their character.

Most contact **metamorphic rocks** remain **fine-grained** and are rather dull to look at. Hornfels is a typical **rock** from contact metamorphism. However, in cracks forced open by the rising magma, hot fluids cooled to form **crystals**. The deposits so formed are called **veins**. Veins are an important source of **metal ores**. (*See also:* **Regional metamorphism**.)

▼ Contact metamorphism—The intrusion of a sill, dike, or magma chamber caused the surrounding rocks to be baked and form a metamorphic zone around the intrusion. The metamorphic zone around a magma chamber (which cools to a batholith) is called a metamorphic aureole.

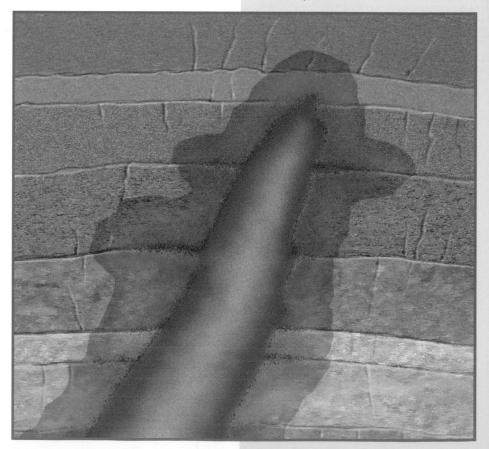

◄ **Copper**—Copper ore.

▼ **Copper**—Pure native copper is orange-red when fresh, but its compounds are often green.

Creep, soil

The gradual downhill, saw-tooth motion of a **clay soil** produced by the shrinking and swelling of clays as they get wet and dry out.

All clay soils shrink as they dry out and swell as they become wet. During the course of a year this may happen many times as a result of alternating rainstorms and periods of dry weather. As the clay soils change shape, gravity causes them to move down a slope.

Soil creep is an extremely slow process. In the past some people have suggested that trees with curved trunks on steep slopes have been pulled over by soil creep. However, this has never been proven.

Cross-bedding

A pattern of deposits in a **sedimentary rock** in which many thin bands of **sediment** lie at an angle to the **bedding planes**. It indicates that the sediment was deposited by wind or flowing water (also called current bedding). The cross-beds deposited by wind are often bigger than those deposited by water.

Copper

An orangy-red soft **metal**. Copper changes to brown when exposed to the air. It was one of the first metals to be used in the ancient world. Its name comes from the Latin *cuprum*, which means "metal of Cyprus," an island in the Mediterranean Sea where the Romans had large copper mines.

Native copper is often found in **basalt rocks** and in **veins** that were once close to **magma** chambers. The shape of a piece of native copper reflects the deep underground fissures in which it was originally deposited. The largest piece of native copper ever found was in Minesota Mine, Michigan. It weighed over 500 tons.

Cotton soil

(*See:* **Vertisol**.)

▼ **Cross bedding**—This occurs when one bed builds forward and cuts across the top of an earlier one.

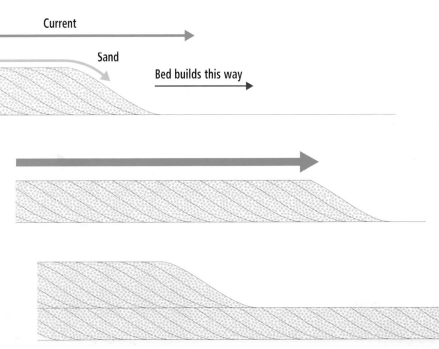

Current

Sand

Bed builds this way

▲ **Crumb structure**—The rounded lumps in this soil show it has a crumb-structured topsoil.

Crumb structure

A **soil** in which the **clay** particles clump together to form irregularly shaped balls. The balls of soil hold together well and resist **erosion**, while allowing good drainage. It is a sign of a stable and fertile topsoil. (*See also:* **Friable** and **Soil structure**.)

Crust

The outermost layer of the Earth, typically 5km thick under the oceans and 50 to 100km thick under continents. It makes up less than 1% of the Earth's volume. (*See also:* **Tectonic plate**.)

Crystal

A **mineral** that has a regular geometric shape and is bounded by smooth, flat faces. Crystals form in six **crystal systems**.

(*See also:* **Cleavage**; **Fracture**; **Gem, gemstones**; **Geode**; **Phenocryst**.)

Crystal system

A group of **crystals** with the same arrangement of axes (*see:* **Axis of symmetry**). There are six crystal systems, as shown below.

(*See also:* **Cubic**; **Hexagonal**; **Orthorhombic**; **Triclinic**.)

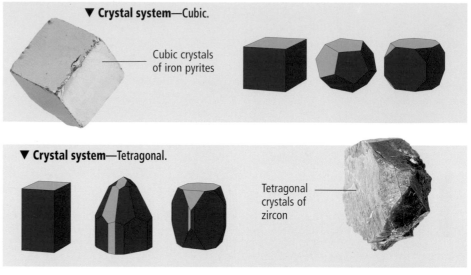

▼ **Crystal system**—Cubic.

Cubic crystals of iron pyrites

▼ **Crystal system**—Tetragonal.

Tetragonal crystals of zircon

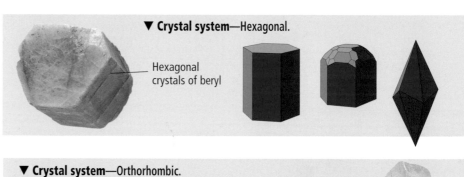

▼ **Crystal system**—Hexagonal.

Hexagonal crystals of beryl

▼ **Crystal system**—Orthorhombic.

Orthorhombic crystals of barite

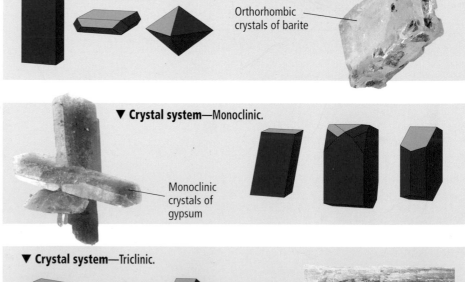

▼ **Crystal system**—Monoclinic.

Monoclinic crystals of gypsum

▼ **Crystal system**—Triclinic.

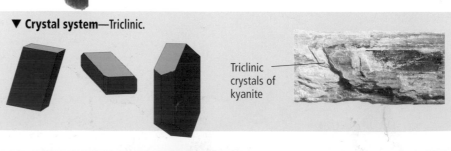

Triclinic crystals of kyanite

Crystalline

A **mineral** that has solidified but has been unable to produce well-formed **crystals**. **Quartz** and **halite** are commonly found as crystalline masses.

Crystallization

The formation of **crystals**.

Cubic

A **crystal system** in which **crystals** have three axes all at right angles to one another and of equal length.

Current bedding

(*See:* **Cross-bedding**.)

Cyclothem

A repeating sequence of **rocks** found in **coal strata**. A cyclothem is formed when the sea level rises and falls by small amounts. The result of the changing sea levels is that a coastal swamp can be easily flooded. This could cause the swamp plants to be buried by a layer of **sand** or **clay**. Then, if the sea level falls a little, a new swamp would form. Many coal-bearing rocks show repeating cycles of this kind. This is why many coal seams are thin, and why coal mines have to exploit many levels in a mine.

D

Desert soil

A poorly formed **soil** in a desert region. Because rainfall is irregular, little material is washed from the **topsoil** to the **subsoil**. With few plants growing in a desert, there is little **humus** in the soil, and the dryness and heat tend to make the humus shrivel up very quickly. Furthermore, when it does rain, the water only seeps a little way into the soil before the heat from the Sun draws it back to the surface,

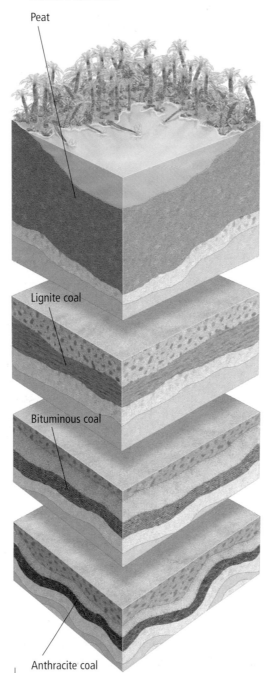

▼ **Cyclothem**—When there are rapid changes of sea level. Cyclothems always include a coal band.

Peat

Lignite coal

Bituminous coal

Anthracite coal

bringing dissolved **minerals** with it. As the water evaporates from the surface, the minerals are left behind and eventually form a salt crust.

Diamond

A form of the element carbon. Diamond is the hardest natural substance known. Pure diamond is a colorless and **transparent mineral**. Diamond is not always colorless; if it contains impurities, it may be a darker color. Some diamonds are almost black.

Diamond is named from the Greek word *adamas*, meaning invincible. Diamonds are formed under immense temperatures and pressures, such as found below volcanoes. The most famous diamond mine, at Kimberley, South Africa, follows an old volcanic pipe for more than two kilometers vertically into the Earth. Diamonds are also found as **placer deposits**.

Diamonds commonly form a shape like two pyramids base to base (a tetrahedron). Jewelers make use of this property when they cut rough diamonds to make jewelry. Each of the faces (called **facets**) is created by splitting the diamond parallel to the faces of its **crystals**.

▼ **Diamond**—These are diamonds in their volcanic rock setting.

▲▶ Dike/Dike swarm—
Dikes occur when igneous rocks break through the surrounding rock. They are usually associated with volcanic activity on a large scale, for example, the splitting of continents. The dike swarms of northern England, Northern Ireland, and Scotland possibly occurred during a phase of the widening of the Atlantic Ocean.

Dike

Dike

Scotland

Northern Ireland

England

Dike

A wall-like sheet of **igneous rock** that cuts across other rocks. (*See also:* **Contact metamorphism** and **Intrusive rock, intrusion.**)

Dike swarm

A collection of hundreds or thousands of parallel **dikes**.

Diorite

An **igneous rock** that forms underground. It has properties between **gabbro** and **granite**; it has the same composition as the **lava** called **andesite**. Diorite is the typical rock of **dikes** and **sills**. It is a medium- to **coarse-grained igneous rock** that contains about two-thirds **feldspar** and one-third dark-colored **minerals**.

Dolomite

A **carbonate mineral** made from calcium and magnesium. This mineral is similar to **calcite**; but because it contains magnesium as well as calcium, it is more resistant to **weathering**. It is opaque, dull white, and is slightly harder than calcite. It is found in **sedimentary rocks**.

E

Eluviation

The washing of **clays** from the **topsoil** to the **subsoil** in slightly **acid soils**. The result is to make the subsoil **heavy** and difficult for farmers to work. It is commonly found in **acid brown soils**. (*See also:* **Alfisol** and **Illuviation**.)

Epoch

A part of a **period** of geological time. In this time a rock **series** can be laid down.

Erode, erosion

The twin processes of breaking down a **rock** (called **weathering**) and then removing the debris (called **transporting**). In some places both processes happen together. For example, in a river a stone being carried by the river may crash into the bank and chip a stone in the bank. This chipping is weathering. The fast-flowing water will then carry this chip away. This is transport. In a **soil**, however, the two parts of the process may be separated by hundreds of years. Rainwater reacts with rock at the base of the soil—weathering. But the soil only moves much later. The word **soil erosion** refers to the washing away of the soil when it is left unprotected, for example, on farmland. This is really accelerated transport, for the weathering part of the erosion process happened long before. (*See also:* **Chemical weathering**; **Gulleying**; **Weathering**.)

Essential mineral

The dominant **mineral** parts of a **rock** that are used to classify it. For example, **quartz** is an essential mineral in **granite** because it is one of the main parts of the rock.

Evaporite

A number of **minerals** are formed by the evaporation of seawater. They are collectively called evaporites, of which the most common are **halite** (salt, sodium chloride) and **gypsum** (calcium sulfate). They are very soft minerals (2 on **Mohs' scale of hardness**) and occur as thick **beds**. They are very soluble minerals, only found in **sedimentary rocks**. (*See also:* **Halide minerals**.)

Extrusive rock, extrusion

An **igneous rock** that has solidified on the surface of the Earth.

The common word for this kind of rock is **lava**.

F

Facet

The cut and polished face of a **gemstone**. Used in describing jewelry. It is not related to the **cleavage** planes of a **mineral**, but is imposed on the gemstone by the skill of the jeweler. (*See also:* **Diamond**.)

Facies

Physical, chemical, or biological variations in a sedimentary **bed** (for example, sandy facies, **limestone** facies). These differences arise because both **clays** and **sand** may be deposited at the same time—clays offshore and sands close to the coast. A **rock** layer made from these deposits may therefore be **shale** (made of clay) in one place, gradually changing to a **sandstone** nearby.

Fault

A break in the Earth's **rocks** due to movements of the **crust**. Faults are of three kinds: **normal**, **reversed**, and transcurrent.

▼ **Evaporite**—Evaporites form naturally in coastal lagoons and in inland basins. This is Nevada.

Feldspars

Silicate minerals. Feldspars are named for the German for "field crystals." About half of all the Earth's crustal **rocks** are made from feldspars. There are two kinds. One kind (**orthoclase** feldspar) is white or gray, and the other kind (**plagioclase** feldspar) is usually pink. You cannot see into a feldspar; it is opaque. But the surface shines (it has a luster like porcelain), and it breaks up into flat-faced blocks.

Feldspars are reasonably hard (6 on **Mohs' scale of hardness**). However, feldspars are easily weathered, and they are the "weak link" in many otherwise resistant rocks, **weathering** into **clay minerals** and allowing the rest of the rock to fall apart. Because they are easily weathered, feldspars are found mostly in **igneous** and **metamorphic rocks**, and are not so common in **sedimentary rocks** (where they have usually been weathered to clay minerals).

▼ **Feldspars**—Feldspars are the most plentiful minerals in igneous rocks, often occurring as large crystals called phenocrysts.

▲ **Fertile soil**—Fertile soils are home to many soil organisms. The birds following this tractor simply wait for the soil to be turned over in order to get an easy meal.

Ferromagnesian minerals

A group of **minerals** that all contain a large proportion of iron and magnesium. In general, they are very difficult to tell apart because they are all green, dark green, or black and often occur only as small **crystals**. Nevertheless, they form a major part of many **igneous** and **metamorphic rocks**, and affect the overall color of the rock. These minerals **weather** easily, and so, while common in igneous and metamorphic rocks, they are not common in **sedimentary rocks**.

Fertile soil

A **soil** in which plants grow well. All plants need a range of "foods" to grow. The "foods" in a soil are called **nutrients**. They are mainly **minerals**, and all are taken up from the water in the soil through the plant roots.

Plants need many nutrients, some in larger quantities than others. They need large amounts of nitrogen, potassium, and calcium. Nitrogen and potassium are released from decaying plant matter (**humus**), which is one reason why adding **compost** or **manure** to a soil is so vital.

Artificial **fertilizers** are also used to add nitrogen and potassium to the soil. Calcium comes from the **weathering** of the **rock** particles in the soil. To replace lost calcium, lime (calcium hydroxide) is added to the soil every few years. (*See also:* **A horizon**.)

Some soils are infertile because they lack just one element, such as zinc or **copper**. Adding special fertilizers to a soil corrects this problem.

Plants cannot usefully take up more nourishment than they need, so adding more fertilizer than necessary is not just a waste of resources, but can actually harm some plants and pollute the rivers that the soil water drains to.

(*For types of fertile soil see:* **Black soil**; **Calcareous soil**; **Chernozem**.)

Fertilizer

An artificial mixture of **nutrients** that plants need for growth. It is added to water and sprayed onto **soils** or spread in the form of powders and pellets. Its main purpose is to improve the levels of nitrogen and potassium in a soil. These two elements are vital for plant growth and high crop yields. (*See also:* **Fertile soil**.)

Fine-grained rocks

Any **rock** that is made mainly of **clay**-sized particles. **Shales** and **mudstones** are the most common **sedimentary rocks** in the world, making up four-fifths of the sedimentary rock.

Flocculation

The grouping together of **clay** particles in a **soil** to make larger clumps that have a size closer to **silt** or **sand**.

Calcium is the key element needed for flocculation. It occurs naturally when there is sufficient calcium in a soil. Clay soils without calcium readily become

waterlogged. It is for this reason, rather than to increase fertility, that farmers with clay soils often add lime (calcium hydroxide) to their fields.

Flood basalt

An eruption of **basalt** that occurs very rarely when a large crack opens in the Earth's crust. Vast volumes of extremely runny **lava** stream over the landscape, often extending to cover millions of square kilometers. The largest of them makes up much of the Deccan region of India, but large flood basalts also occur in the Columbia-Snake basin of the northwestern United States.

Foliation

A sheetlike pattern of **rock** (usually **schist**) that looks like the pages in a book.

Formation

A collection of related **rock** layers or **beds**. A group of related beds makes a member; a group of related members makes up a formation. Formations are often given location names, for example, Toroweap Formation (a dominant formation in the Grand Canyon, Arizona). In the case of the Toroweap Formation the members are mainly **limestone** beds.

Fossil

The remains of living things that have been preserved in **rocks**. Fossils are used to find out about ancient environments, how rocks formed, and what the Earth's history was like. They are also used to help find **petroleum** deposits and have been invaluable in tracing the history of life on Earth.

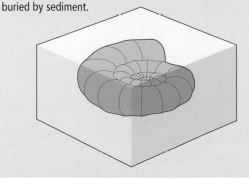

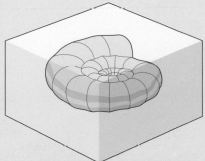

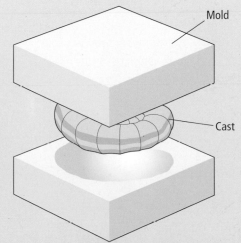

◄▼ **Fossil**—Fossils are common in rocks. Certain calm conditions allow the almost perfect preservation of large specimens. They are important for the dating of rocks and also to indicate the environmental conditions under which the rocks formed.

The diagram below shows the stages in making a cast or mold of a fossil.

3—Solutions passing through the sediment deposit minerals in the mold to produce a cast of the skeleton (and sometimes also the soft parts) of the original creature. Both mold and cast provide a record of the fossil and may be found in rocks.

Mold

Cast

2—The soft parts, and possibly the skeleton as well, are dissolved away, leaving a mold.

1—The dead animal is buried by sediment.

Fracture

A substantial break across a **rock**. Some **crystals** break irregularly, rather than in a single direction. This indicates that the crystal has no special lines of weakness. A curved fracture is known as a conchoidal fracture. Flint and glass show conchoidal fracture. (*See also:* **Fracture zone** and **Slaty cleavage**.)

Fracture zone

A region of **rock** in which **fractures** are common. Fracture zones are particularly common in folded rock and near **faults**. (*See also:* **Normal fault** and **Reversed fault**).

Fracture zones are places where rocks have been broken and are more liable to **erode**. Fracture zones are often connected with bands of low land. River valleys sometimes follow fracture zones.

Friable

Used to describe **soil** that naturally breaks up into small clumps (**crumb structure**). It refers to a **loamy** soil or a **clay** soil with a good calcium content.

Fuel

Any material that can be used to produce heat energy. The main fuels in use today are called **fossil** fuels—**coal**, oil, and natural gas. They are called fossil fuels because they were formed in the geological past and are not forming in such abundance today.

G

Gabbro

An **alkaline igneous rock**, typically showing dark-colored **crystals**. It is made of the same minerals as **basalt**, but it has large

▲ Galena—An important lead-bearing ore.

crystals because it solidified slowly deep underground.

Although gabbro makes up a thick layer below the basalt that covers the ocean floor, it is rare to find gabbro on land. Outcrops of gabbro mainly occur where parts of ancient ocean plates have been buckled upward and made into mountains.

(*See also:* **Basic rock** and **Hornblende**.)

▼ Garnet—Garnets are red minerals often found in metamorphic rocks.

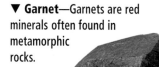

Galena

This **mineral**, lead sulfide, is often found as small cubic **crystals**. It has some features of a **metal**, being bright and shiny, but others of a nonmetal. Like salt, it is brittle.

Galena is found in places that have experienced volcanic activity. It is associated with zones from which miners collect other **ores**, such as **silver** and tin.

It is also found in **limestone** and **dolomite rocks** through which heated waters have passed—that is, it can be a **hydrothermal** mineral. Galena comes from the Greek *galena*, meaning lead ore.

Gangue

The unwanted **minerals** found in a **metal ore**. Common gangue minerals include **quartz** and **calcite**. They often make up the majority of a mineral **vein**.

Garnet

Olivine-type **minerals**—but with a red color. They form **crystals** that can often be large, especially in **metamorphic rock**. The crystals typically have 12 faces.

Gem, gemstone

A **mineral**, usually in **crystal** form, that is regarded as having particular beauty and value. **Diamonds**, rubies, and sapphires are examples of gems. (*See also:* **Facet**.)

Geode

A hollow lump of **rock** (nodule) that often contains **crystals**.

Geology

The scientific study of the Earth and its **rocks**.

▲ **Geode**—A very ordinary nodule may harbor a spectacular interior of crystals. These are amethysts.

Geosyncline

A large, slowly subsiding region, often on the edge of a continent, that is filling in with huge amounts of **sediment**. The word means "Earth-sized trench." Most geosynclines are below sea level (for example, the East Coast of the United States is a geosyncline), but some (for example, the Ganges Plain) lie within continents. The rocks in a geosyncline may run many tens of thousands of meters. Many of them are **graywackes**. When they are eventually lifted, they form mountain belts. **Fossils** and **sedimentary rocks** are found in even the world's highest mountains because they were once geosynclines.

Gley

A gray, **waterlogged soil** layer in which the iron **minerals** have lost some of their oxygen. As a result, the normal rusty brown color of a soil is changed to gray.

▼ **Gley**—Gley soils have gray horizons as a result of frequent waterlogging.

Water-tolerant plants

Dark-brown to black waterlogged topsoil.

Brown subsoil with gray blotches.

Gray parent material

▼ **Gneiss**—Gneiss represents the most extreme form of metamorphism. The rocks are coarse and banded, and quite often pink, as here in the Sangre de Cristo Mountains, Colorado.

Gneiss

A **metamorphic rock** showing large **grains** and very prominent banding. A gneiss is formed within a mountain system where there are both high temperatures and very high pressure. Many gneisses were formerly **granites**. Large crystals grow in some gneisses. They are called augen gneiss, from the German *augen*, meaning eyes. (*See also:* **Regional metamorphism**.)

Gold

A soft, golden yellow **metal** that is usually uncombined with other metals. It is one of the heaviest metals that is common. Gold is often found in **veins** that were once close to **magma** chambers, alongside **silver** and **copper**.

Grain

A particle of a **rock** or **mineral**. (*See also:* **Clast**.)

Granite

An **acidic**, **igneous rock** formed deep below the surface of the Earth, mainly in the **magma** chambers that once fed volcanoes. Because this material was insulated from the surface, it cooled slowly, giving time for **crystals** to form.

The biggest crystals in a granite are usually **feldspar**. They make the gray, white, or pink opaque shapes in a granite. Black **micas** form much smaller crystals (*see:* **Biotite**). A mass of **crystalline quartz** (looking like grayish glass) fills in the spaces between the feldspar and mica crystals.

Granites are easily recognized and colorful rocks. Large masses of granite are found in **batholiths**. (*See also:* **Acid soil**; **Arkose**; **Rhyolite**.)

Gray-brown soil

Soils of the cool humid regions, often found under coniferous forest or heath. They are midway between **brown soils** and **podzols**. They have poorly decomposing acidic **humus** surface layers. Rainwater passing through the humus carries acids into the soil. The acids react with iron from the **topsoil**, making it soluble and allowing it to be washed into the **subsoil**. This leaves the topsoil grayer in color. (*See also:* **Acid soil**; **Brown soil**; **Podzol**.)

Graywacke

A type of **sedimentary rock** formed by an underwater landslide. All of the particles in a graywacke are arranged chaotically. Graywackes are important sedimentary rocks in mountain chains. Before being lifted up into mountains, they formed in **geosynclines**.

▼ **Granite**—Granite is typified by a mixture of large pink or gray feldspar crystals and small black biotite crystals set in a ground of glassy quartz.

Pink (plagioclase) feldspar

Quartz

Black biotite

Grit

Grains larger than **sand** (2mm across) but smaller than stones. Grit stones look like coarse **sandstones**. Grit stones were once valued as grinding stones and were often used in flour mills. They are still used today for producing "stone-ground" flour.

Gulleying

A form of accelerated **soil** transport that mainly occurs in places where people have stripped off the natural vegetation and left it exposed to heavy rainstorms. As the rainwater runs off the surface, it gathers speed until it can begin to carry soil particles along. First, small channels called **rills** form. Rills are shallow enough that they can later be plowed out. If rills combine to make deeper channels that cannot be plowed out, they are called gullies. (*See also:* **Erode, erosion** and **Soil erosion**.)

Gypsum

A mineral made of calcium sulfate. Gypsum is soft (hardness 2 on the **Mohs' scale**) and **translucent** white. It is an **evaporite** mineral.

H

Halide minerals

A group of **minerals**—for example, **halite** (rock salt)—that contain a halogen element (elements similar to chlorine) bonded with another element. Many are **evaporite** minerals.

▲ **Halite**—Crystalline halite is called rock salt.

Halite

A **mineral** made of sodium chloride. It is normally called rock salt. It occurs in thick **beds** that represent former dry lake or lagoon beds. (*See also:* **Chemical rock**; **Crystalline**; **Evaporite**.)

Heavy soil

A **soil** that is difficult to cultivate because it is dominated by **clays**. Heavy soils are improved by treating them with **manure** and calcium. Both of these materials help the clay form clumps (*see:* **Crumb structure**; **Flocculation**) and so drain better. Heavy soils may also need to be drained.

Hematite

Iron **oxide**, one of the main **ores** of iron. It is found in **igneous**, **metamorphic**, and **sedimentary** **rocks**. The word hematite comes from the Greek *haimatites*, meaning color of blood. Hematite is the most widespread form of iron ore. (*See also:* **Botryoidal**.)

Hexagonal

A **crystal system** in which the **crystals** have three axes all at 120° to one another and of equal length (*see:* **Axis of symmetry**). Beryl is a **mineral** of this system.

Horizon, soil

A distinctive layer in a **soil**. It is a word used by soil scientists. Gardeners use the words **topsoil** and **subsoil** to refer to **A horizons** and **B horizons** respectively.

The rock or other material on which a soil forms is called the **parent material** and is designated as the **C horizon**.

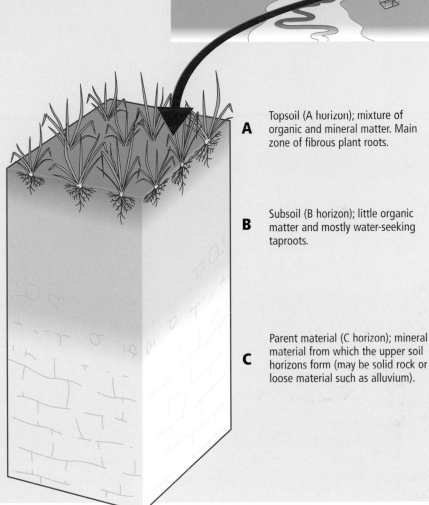

▼ **Horizon, soil**—Soils are divided into layers called horizons. The main ones are A, B, and C, sometimes subdivided to describe important features.

A — Topsoil (A horizon); mixture of organic and mineral matter. Main zone of fibrous plant roots.

B — Subsoil (B horizon); little organic matter and mostly water-seeking taproots.

C — Parent material (C horizon); mineral material from which the upper soil horizons form (may be solid rock or loose material such as alluvium).

Hornblende

A dark-green **silicate mineral** containing sodium, potassium, calcium, magnesium, iron, and aluminum. Hornblende is a common mineral in **rocks** such as **basalt** and **gabbro**. (*See also:* **Ferromagnesium mineral**.)

Humus

Decomposed **organic matter** in a **soil**. Humus is vital for two reasons. First, it contains large amounts of nitrogen and potassium, which are essential **nutrients** for growing plants. Second, it contains threads of sticky substances that bind soil particles together and keep the fine **clay** particles from clogging up the soil or from being blown away in a strong wind. A soil should have at least 1% humus to be **fertile**. (*See also:* **Alfisol**; **Black soil**; **Chernozem**; **Compost**; **Crumb structure**; **Moder**; **Mor**; **Mulch**.)

Hydrothermal

A change brought about in a **rock** or **mineral** due to the action of superheated mineral-rich fluids, usually water.

When molten rock forces its way to the surface, it includes the sticky material that will later become a volcanic eruption and many more liquid mixtures that can easily force their way into small cracks in the neighboring rocks. They are called hydrothermal (hot-water) liquids. They contain rich concentrations of **metals**. When they later cool and solidify in the surrounding rocks, they form rich mineral deposits that can be worked for metals such as **gold**, **silver**, **copper**, zinc, and lead (*see:* **Galena**).

I

Igneous rock

Rock formed when **magma** cools and solidifies. Igneous rocks are found in volcanic rocks such as **lava** and **ash** and once-buried rocks such as **dikes** and **batholiths**. **Granite** is the most common igneous rock on land. It forms when magma cools in a batholith. The most common igneous rock of all is **basalt**. It is mainly found on the floors of the world's oceans, but also makes dikes and **sills** on land.

(*For types of igneous rock see:* **Acid rock**; **Andesite**; **Diorite**; **Extrusive rock, extrusion**; **Feldspar**; **Gabbro**; **Granite**; **Plutonic rock**; **Porphyry, porphyritic rock**; **Rhyolite**.)

Illuviation

The process of depositing **clays** washed from the **topsoil** into the **subsoil**. It tends to occur in slightly **acid soils** and where there is too little calcium or **humus** in the soil to hold the clay particles together (preventing **flocculation**). Soils with lots of clay in the subsoil tend to **waterlog** easily and be difficult to work. (*See also:* **Acid brown soil** and **Eluviation**.)

Impermeable

A **rock** or **soil** that will not allow a liquid to pass through it.

Combinations of permeable and impermeable rocks produce springs and trap water and **petroleum**.

A band of impermeable rock is called an **aquiclude** (while a band of **permeable rock** is called an **aquifer**). An impermeable rock above an aquifer can trap water underground. If a well is drilled through an impermeable rock, water will gush up from the underlying aquifer.

If an impermeable rock lies above a permeable rock containing natural gas and oil, the petroleum will be trapped. The impermeable rock is then called a **cap rock**. If a well is drilled through the cap rock, natural gas and crude oil will gush to the surface.

If an impermeable rock lies below an aquifer, then the water will be stored above the aquiclude, and a spring will be formed wherever the edges of the rocks are exposed at the surface. Spring lines thus show approximately where permeable and impermeable rock meet.

Impurities

Small amounts of elements or compounds in a **mineral**.

Infiltration

The process of water sinking through the surface of the **soil**. Once the water has entered the soil, it spreads through the soil (*see:* **Permeable soil**).

If the soil surface has been trampled or crushed by heavy machinery, the infiltration of water may be low, even though the permeability of the soil below the crushed layer may be high. Soils with a surface crust formed by splashing rain will also have low infiltration rates.

Inorganic matter

The **mineral matter** in a **soil**.

Intrusive rock, intrusion

Rocks that have formed from cooling **magma** that has forced its way through other rocks.

The main types of intrusion are **batholiths**, **bosses**, **laccoliths**, **sills**, and **dikes**.

Batholiths are huge bodies of **granite** that were formerly magma chambers supplying volcanoes. As magma forced its way from these chambers into weaknesses in the surrounding rock, it created many kinds of intrusion. Sheets of **igneous rock** formed by prying the surrounding rocks apart are called sills; those that cut across the surrounding rocks and form wall-like sheets are called dikes.

▶ **Latosol**—This is a latosol soil from Queensland in Australia. It is very deep, and the red color indicates that it is enriched with iron. On exposure to air some latosols become very hard and form laterites.

▼ **Laterite**—Laterites can contain iron nodules.

▶ **Iron pan**—An iron pan can be seen as a thin orange line in some podzol soils.

Iron pan

A layer of iron-rich **soil** that lies at the top of a **B horizon** in a **podzol** soil. An iron pan is usually **impermeable** and so holds up water above it. (*See also:* **Laterite**.)

Irrigation

The artificial watering of land in order to help it produce better crops. There are many irrigation methods, including flooding the land (as in paddy fields), using sprays and sprinklers, and drip feeding the roots of plants using pipes laid across the fields.

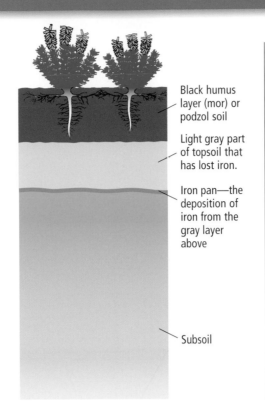

Black humus layer (mor) or podzol soil

Light gray part of topsoil that has lost iron.

Iron pan—the deposition of iron from the gray layer above

Subsoil

J

Joint

A significant crack between blocks of **rock**, normally used to mean patterns of cracks. (*See also:* **Bedding planes** and **Fractures**.)

L

Laccolith

A lens-shaped body of **intrusive igneous rock** with a dome-shaped upper surface and a flat bottom surface. It is a relatively uncommon feature.

Laterite

A former **soil** layer that has become exposed by the **erosion** of the **topsoil**. Most laterites were formed in tropical environments over iron-rich **rocks**. The main cause of a laterite is the **leaching** of iron from hillside soils and its transport through the soil to places where it becomes concentrated, usually in the **subsoils** of soils close to a valley floor.

The iron content of a laterite layer can be extraordinarily high. While it remains part of the subsoil, the iron-rich layer stays soft; but if the topsoil is **eroded** away, the subsoil dries out to a rocklike substance. Laterites are so rich in iron they have been used as iron **ore** supplies for iron and steel plants. (*See also:* **Latosol**.)

Latosol

A tropical rain-forest **soil** containing a **subsoil** very rich in iron. If the **topsoil** is eroded away, the subsoil of a latosol may form into a **laterite**.

Lava

Molten rock that flows over the surface of the Earth or the solidified **rock** formed from flowing lava.

Lava flows from volcanoes (*see:* **Viscous, viscosity**). Most lava is made of **basalt**. Basalt has a very low **silica** content, and when molten, basaltic lava can be very runny, flowing as rivers or flooding across the landscape as sheets. When basalt cools, it turns black.

Lava can have a smooth surface, in which case it is known as pahoehoe lava, or it can be broken and cinderlike, in which case it is called aa lava (named for places in Hawaii). Lava need not be solid rock and may contain lava tubes, tunnels where lava once flowed below a solidified surface.

If lava erupts under water, it cools very quickly. As a result, the lava forms a succession of pillow-shaped masses of rock. Once one pillow has been created, the pressure of lava breaks it off, and new liquid lava flows into the sea, solidifying to make another pillow along the crack where the lava is erupting. Finding pillow shapes in lava tells you that the lava erupted under water.

Very occasionally supervolcanoes erupt and send out vast volumes of lava across the landscape. No one has ever witnessed such a flow, but there is plenty of evidence to prove that they have happened in the past. Supervolcanoes produced the giant sheets of lava called plateau lavas (*see:* **Flood basalt**). It is thought that during one of these massive eruptions lava flowed over thousands of square kilometers of land within just a few days or weeks. The Columbia-Snake basin in the northwestern United States is one example; the Deccan

▲ **Lava**—Basaltic lava congeals on the surface into a black rock that looks like molten tar, while molten lava flows underneath in lava tubes, often for many kilometers.

plateau of India is another.

(*See also:* **Andesite**; **Extrusive rock, extrusion**; **Igneous rock**; **Obsidian**; **Scoria**; **Vesicle**.)

Law of superposition

The principle that younger **rock** is usually laid down on older rock.

Layered rock

One form of **sedimentary rock**. Most of the pieces of **rock** carried by rivers, glaciers, and waves eventually settle out in the sea as **sediment**. The sediment builds up in layers.

Leach, leaching

The removal of material in solution from the upper part of a **soil**. It only happens in **acid soils**. Signs of strong leaching are found in changes in color within the **topsoil** and **subsoil**. Iron helps give most soils their **color**. A soil without leaching is mostly rusty brown. When iron is leached, the topsoil becomes a pale gray, while the subsoil becomes bright orange and may even develop an **iron pan**. (*See also:* **Laterite** and **Podzol**.) **Clays** are never leached; they are washed down through the soil (by **eluviation**) instead.

Leaf litter

The dead leaves that lie on the surface of a **soil**. Once they rot and are incorporated into the soil by earthworms and other soil life, they will become **humus**. (*See also:* **Mull**.)

Light soil

A **soil** that contains a large proportion of **sand** or **silt** and relatively little **clay**. A light soil may blow away in a strong wind and will need protection. The Dust Bowl disaster on the Great Plains of North America in the

1930s was the result of light soils blowing. The same happens in Victoria, Australia, creating dust-laden winds called a buster or brickfielder. (*Contrast with:* **Heavy soil**.)

Limestone

A **sedimentary rock** in which more than half the material is calcium **carbonate** (**calcite**).

There are a wide variety of limestones. Some, like **chalk**, are quite soft, while others, like so-called mountain limestone, are so hard they can be used as the foundations for roads.

All limestones react easily with acids (*see:* **Chemical weathering** and **Weathering**) and are therefore much more readily **eroded** in humid climates than in desert climates. In a desert limestones behave as just another hard rock, while in humid climates limestones may erode chemically faster than other rocks.

Many limestones are gray and appear to be massive. Others have **fractured** into blocks. If these fractured blocks are exposed at the surface, water can seep into them and dissolve the faces of the blocks. These bare surfaces with widened cracks are called limestone pavements.

Solution does not stop at the surface. It also occurs below the surface and affects wherever water flows through limestone. In time huge amounts of limestone can be eroded away, leaving an underground landscape of caves and tunnels.

Limestones are formed in many different environments. Some appear in seas that contain very

Limestone fossil

Limestone rock

Crystals of calcite

▲ **Limestone**—Limestone can be found as rock, as fossils, and as the mineral calcite.

little **sediment.** In this case the limestone rock is almost pure white. Others emerge in a sea in which there is a large amount of **clay.** The combination of calcium carbonate and clay creates a gray limestone.

The calcium carbonate of most limestones comes from the skeletons of sea organisms. Chalk is entirely made from the skeletons of microscopic sea creatures. Many limestones also contain remains of larger creatures such as corals, mollusks, and sea urchins. These **fossils** can all be used to identify the rocks.

When cut and polished, hard limestones containing large fossils can be extremely decorative and are used for floors of buildings.

(*See also:* **Formation**.)

Lithosphere

That part of the Earth's **crust** and upper mantle which is brittle and makes up the **tectonic plates**.

Loam

A **soil texture** containing approximately equal proportions of **sand**, **silt**, and **clay** particles. Loamy soils have good drainage (from the sand) and good fertility (from the clay). Loam is often considered to be an ideal soil texture for gardening and farming. (*See also:* **Friable**.)

Lode

A mining term for a **rock** containing many rich **ore**-bearing **minerals**. Prospectors often looked for a rich **vein** that was the source of fragments of **metal** they found in nearby rivers. They called it "the mother lode." Lode is used in a way similar to vein.

Loess

A name for a **silt**-rich loose material that blankets the hard rocks in some parts of the world. It is a deposit that formed at the end of the last Ice Age, when vast tracts of land were released from under the ice. Glacial **erosion** naturally produces huge amounts of silt. Winds can carry the silt from newly exposed areas to settle elsewhere. This is the material called loess.

Large loess spreads are found in North America and China. Loess is an example of a material that geologists call a **superficial**, or **unconsolidated**, **deposit**.

(*See also:* **Parent material**.)

Luster

The way in which a mineral reflects light. Used as a test for identifying **minerals**.

M

Magma

The molten material that comes from the Earth's mantle, and that cools to form **igneous rocks**.

▼ **Magma**—Magma is found in large chambers below volcanoes. It is the source of lava (shown orange) or dikes and sills (shown black), as well as the heat source for geothermal power supplies (indicated by the blue arrow).

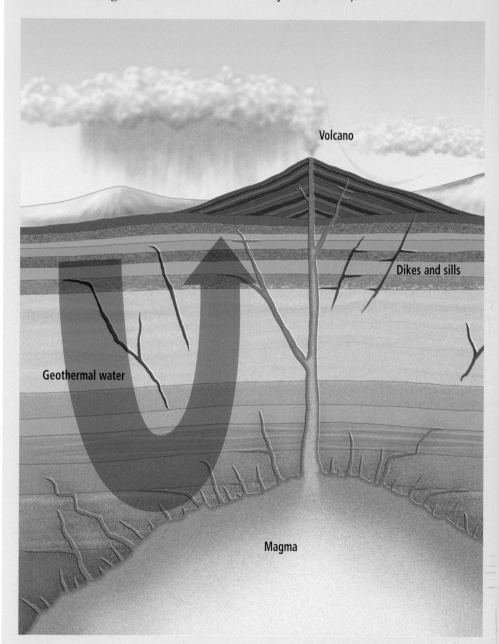

Volcano

Dikes and sills

Geothermal water

Magma

Manure

Organic material made from the waste of animals or decaying plants. As it breaks down, it forms **humus**, which is vital to **soil** fertility and **structure** (*see:* **Fertile soil**).

Marble

Carbonate sedimentary rocks that have been subjected to heat, pressure, and **hydrothermal** fluids. Because **calcite** and **dolomite minerals** are uniform in character, the effect of **regional**

metamorphism is not to produce a parallel arrangement of the **crystals**, as happens in **slate** or **schist**, but rather to fuse the entire rock together and to increase the **grain** size. The metamorphic character of the rock is often best shown by the smeared-out color impurities that give the rock its "marbling."

Metal

One of a group of elements that are found in most **minerals**. Metals make up three-quarters of all elements. Common metals found in minerals include calcium (found, for example, in **calcite**), sodium (found, for example, in salt), and iron (found, for example, in most dark-colored minerals such as **augite** and **hornblende**). A few metals can be found uncombined, of which **copper**, **silver**, and **gold** are examples.

Metamorphic aureole

The region surrounding a **batholith** that was affected by the heat from a former **magma** chamber. This region contains heat-baked **rocks** and also **veins** rich in **minerals**. It is an important place for recovering many **metals**. (*See also:* **Contact metamorphism**.)

▶ **Metamorphic rock**—This is garnetiferous mica schist, a typical metamorphic rock. The wavy layers called foliation are easy to see. They are the result of pressure and high temperatures. The heat has also caused garnets to form.

Metamorphic rock

Any **rock** (for example, **schist**, **gneiss**) that was formed from a preexisting rock by heat and pressure.

Metamorphic rocks vary greatly depending on the amount of heat and pressure applied and on the material from which they developed.

The least altered metamorphic rock is a **shale** that has simply been compressed so hard that the **clay crystals** have changed into tiny **mica** flakes. This produces a rock called **slate**.

If a shale rock is baked by being buried deep underground, it changes into a dull brown rock called hornfels.

Moderate heat and pressure produce a slightly lustrous rock called phyllite.

More intense heat and pressure (as found deep inside a mountain chain) produce **schist** and **gneiss**.

In the most intensively metamorphosed rocks (schist and gneiss) new crystals form. Some of these crystals can be very large. **Garnets** typically grow in both schists and gneisses. (*See also:* **Contact metamorphism**; **Regional metamorphism**; **Tectonic plate**.)

▼ **Metamorphic rock**—How a granite might be changed by metamorphism. Notice the crystals have completely disappeared, and instead the rock contains contorted bands of light and dark minerals.

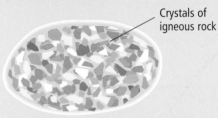

Crystals of igneous rock

Bands of crystalline rock containing light and dark minerals.

Meteorite

A large chunk of **rock** moving through space. When meteorites collide with the Earth, they can do substantial damage. Meteor Crater in Arizona is the world's best-known example of a meteorite striking the Earth.

Micas

Sheetlike **minerals** that break up into flakes. There are many micas, but the most common are brown, white, or colorless **muscovite** and black **biotite**. Micas are soft (2–3 on **Mohs' scale of hardness**) but quite resistant to **weathering**. They are flat, platelike **crystals** that normally form small, shiny specks in a **rock**. They are very common in **igneous rocks**, in many **metamorphic rocks**, especially **schists**, and also in some **sandstones**.

Mineral

From a **geologist's** point of view a mineral is any naturally occurring inorganic substance of definite chemical composition (for example, **calcite**, calcium **carbonate**).

From a mining point of view a mineral is any useful resource extracted from the ground by mining (including **metal ores**, **coal**, oil, gas, **rocks**, and so on).

(*See also:* **Luster; Mineral environment; Mineralization; Reniform; Skarn; Streak; Transluscent; Transparent.**)

(*For groups of minerals see:* **Carbonate minerals; Crystal; Crystalline; Essential minerals; Evaporite; Ferromagnesium minerals; Gem, gemstones; Halide minerals; Micas; Native metal; Olivine; Ore mineral; Oxide minerals; Rock-forming mineral; Silica, silicate; Sulfides.**)

(*For individual minerals see:* **Augite; Bauxite; Beryl; Biotite;**

Coal; Copper; Diamond; Dolomite; Galena; Garnet; Gold; Gypsum; Halite; Hematite; Hornblende; Muscovite; Pyrite; Quartz; Silver; Sulfur; Talc.)

Mineral environment

The place where a **mineral** or a group of associated minerals formed. Mineral environments include **igneous**, **sedimentary**, and **metamorphic rocks**.

Mineral matter

The particles of **rock** in a **soil**. The same as **inorganic matter**.

Mineralization

The formation of **minerals** within a **rock**.

Moder

A dark layer of decomposing leaves and other materials that forms on the surface of slightly **acid soils**. It tends to be found in cool, humid climates in upland areas. It is intermediate between **mull** and **mor**.

Mohs' scale of hardness

A relative scale developed to organize **minerals** in order of hardness. Any mineral on the scale will scratch any mineral lower down the scale and be scratched by any mineral higher on the scale. The hardest is 10 (**diamond**), and the softest is 1 (**talc**).

Moisture, soil

The amount of water held between the particles of **soil**. When a soil holds all the moisture it can, it is said to be **waterlogged**

▶ **Mohs' scale of hardness**—This scale uses common minerals to produce a comparative scale to test all minerals. The softest is number **1** on the scale, and the hardest is **10**.

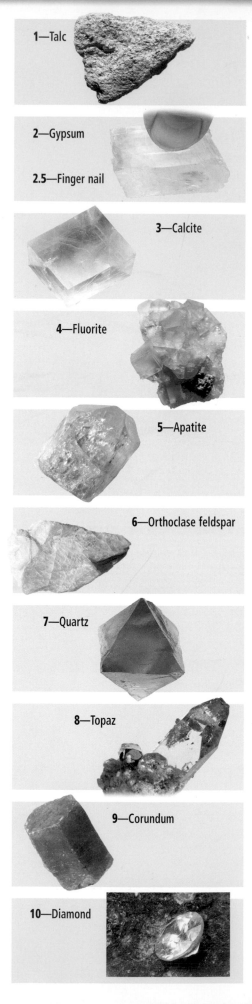

1—Talc

2—Gypsum

2.5—Finger nail

3—Calcite

4—Fluorite

5—Apatite

6—Orthoclase feldspar

7—Quartz

8—Topaz

9—Corundum

10—Diamond

or saturated. If waterlogging continues for some time, the color of the soil will change to gray, and the soil will be **gleyed.**

Mor

A thin, dark layer of **humus,** less decomposed than **moder,** that forms on the surface of very **acid soils.** So few **soil** creatures can live in this cold, acid environment that it rots very slowly. Very little of it gets incorporated into the **topsoil.** Acid water drains from and **leaches minerals** from the topsoil. Mor humus is commonly found as the upper layer on **podzol** soils.

Mountain soil

Soils that form under conditions of cold weather at high altitudes.

The main **weathering** process in these environments is frost shattering, which is why mountain soils contain large amounts of shattered **rock.** Cool conditions do not favor **chemical weathering,** and so few **clay** particles are produced. This makes soil development poor, and mountain soils do not have soil **horizons.**

Plants growing in mountain soils have to adapt to this environment, as do plants in a desert—by growing deep taproots, woody stems, and small leaves, and by having the ability to grow quickly when conditions are right.

Muck

A North American term for **peat soils.** They are saturated with water for many months of the year. They are found particularly on flat, poorly drained uplands and places in northerly latitudes. The main plants growing in these areas are water-tolerant firs, together with sedges, rushes, and mosses. Their remains build up on the surface as muck.

Mudstone

A **fine-grained,** massive **rock** formed by the compaction of mud. Similar to **shale** but often somewhat softer.

Mulch

A thick layer of **manure,** or leaves, or other kind of plant matter that is laid over the **soil** surface to keep in **moisture** and prevent weeds from growing.

Mull

The decomposing **leaf litter** that forms on neutral and **alkaline soils.** This material is alive with **soil** creatures that quickly break it down and incorporate it into the **topsoil.**

Muscovite

A brown form of mica. The name muscovite comes from Muscovy glass because it was once used instead of glass in Russia. As thin sheets it is almost **transparent** and is known as isinglass. It is sometimes used for furnace windows.

N

Native metal

A **metal** that occurs uncombined with any other element. Native metals include **gold,** platinum, **silver,** and **copper.**

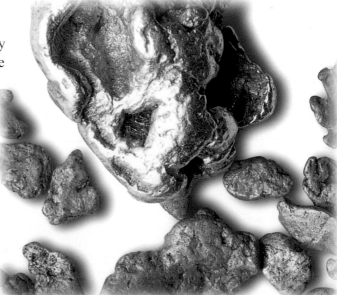

▶ **Native metal**—Gold is one of the best-known native metals, often found in the beds of mountain streams. Native metals such as gold and silver have been sought by prospectors for centuries.

Normal fault

A **fault** in which one rock face has slipped down across the face of another. It is the most common kind of fault and results from tension in the **crust.** (*See also:* **Reversed fault.**)

▲ **Muscovite**—Muscovite is a light brown form of mica.

Nutrient

Any element or compound found in a **soil** that is essential for healthy plant growth. **Humus** is naturally rich in nutrients. **Fertilizers** are applied to soils to provide extra amounts of nutrients.

O

Obsidian

Glassy **rocks** often associated with the rapid cooling of very sticky **lava**. Obsidian has a low water content and a high **silica** content. It normally forms on the surface of a **rhyolite** type of **magma**.

This kind of magma, although also very acidic and with a high silica content, contains about 10% water, which keeps it mobile. When the magma reaches the surface, the water boils off. As a result, the magma increases rapidly in stickiness and, at the same time, cools. These are the conditions that produce volcanic glass. Obsidian is, therefore, the material that normally forms on top of rhyolite lava flows. You cannot see through the glass because it contains too many emerging crystals. As a result, there is no clear path for light to pass through.

Olivine

The name of a group of magnesium iron **silicate minerals** that have an olive color. They mostly form small **crystals** in dark-colored **igneous** and **metamorphic rocks**. (*See also:* **Garnet**.)

▲ **Obsidian**—One of the few forms of natural glass.

Ore

A **rock** containing enough useful **metal** or **fuel** to be worth mining. The amount of waste rock (**gangue**) that can be tolerated depends on the price that can be obtained for the metal or fuel. In the case of **gold**, uranium, and molybdenum, for example, just a few grams per ton of rock can make the ore worth mining. In the case of iron ore the iron content normally has to be above a third to make it worth mining. (*See also:* **Lode**; **Ore mineral**; **Pegmatite**.)

Ore mineral

A **mineral** that occurs in sufficient quantity to be mined for its **metal**. The compound must also be easy to process. (*See also:* **Sulfides**.)

Organic matter

Any material in a **soil** that comes from a living thing. Organic matter is often found on the surface as **leaf litter** or **moder**, **mor**, and **mull**. Inside the soil it is found as **humus**. (*See also:* **Brown soil, brown earth**.)

Orthoclase

The form of **feldspar** that is often pink. It contains more potassium than **plagioclase** feldspar.

Orthorhombic

A **crystal system** in which **crystals** have three axes all at right angles to one another but of unequal length (*see:* **Axis of symmetry**).

Outcrop

An exposure of a **rock** at the surface of the Earth. Outcrops are most noticeable at the coast, when they make cliffs, or in mountains where no **soil** forms.

◄ **Outcrop**—This is a place where a hard band of sandstone occurs, or crops out, at the surface. A soft band of shale outcrops below it, but shale, being a soft rock, does not produce such dramatic outcrops.

Overburden

The unwanted layer(s) of **rock** above an **ore** or **coal** body.

Oxide minerals

A group of **minerals** in which oxygen is attached to a **metal** (for example, iron oxide—**hematite**—and aluminum oxide—**bauxite**).

P

Parent material

The **rock** or other material on which a **soil** develops. There are many kinds of parent material in addition to solid rock. Alluvium—the material deposited by a river—is a common parent material, as is wind-blown **loess** and the bouldery clay material called till, left when ice sheets melt away. Most soils north of about 48°N are formed on till rather than on solid rock. (*See also:* **C horizon**.)

▶ **Parent material**—A soil develops from solid rock, river alluvium, or some other parent material. In this photograph a brown soil is shown developed on a slate parent material. The start of the parent material is marked by the tip of the trowel blade.

Peat

An accumulation of decomposed plant remains. It occurs when water does not drain away, and so the normal processes of decay cannot occur. Peat can be cut and used as a **fuel**. (*See also:* **Muck**.)

Pegmatite

An **igneous rock** (for example, a **dike**) of extremely coarse **crystals**. Pegmatites are a rich source of **ores** and **mineral crystals** of great size and value.

Percolation

The downward movement of water through a **soil** or **rock**. A **permeable rock** is one in which percolation can occur.

Period

A large unit of geological time. It begins and ends with some easily recorded and dramatic change in the **rocks**, such as a mass extinction of living things. Geological periods last for tens of millions of years and have names like Jurassic and Permian. The rocks associated with a geological period make up a geological system. (*See also:* **Epoch**.)

Permeable rock

A **rock** that will allow a fluid (water, crude oil, or natural gas) to pass through it. Permeable rocks that contain water are called **aquifers**. This is not the same as **porous**, which simply means a rock or soil containing small cavities or holes. To be permeable, the **pores** in a rock must connect to allow a liquid to pass through. (*See also:* **Impermeable** and **Percolation**.)

Permeable soil

A **soil** that lets water pass through it easily. It is the equivalent to well-drained soil. Most soils that contain **sand** and are rich in **humus** and calcium are well drained.

Petroleum

The carbon-rich, and mostly liquid, mixture produced by animal and plant remains that have been buried and transformed by heat and pressure over long periods of time.

Petroleum is found in many **sedimentary rocks**. The liquid part of petroleum is called oil; the gaseous part is known as natural gas. Petroleum is an important fossil **fuel**. (*See also:* **Impermeable**; **Petroleum field**; **Reservoir rock**.)

Petroleum field

A region from which **petroleum** can be recovered.

▼ **Petroleum**—Petroleum occurs naturally in a number of rock structures where it becomes trapped. These are shown on this diagram.

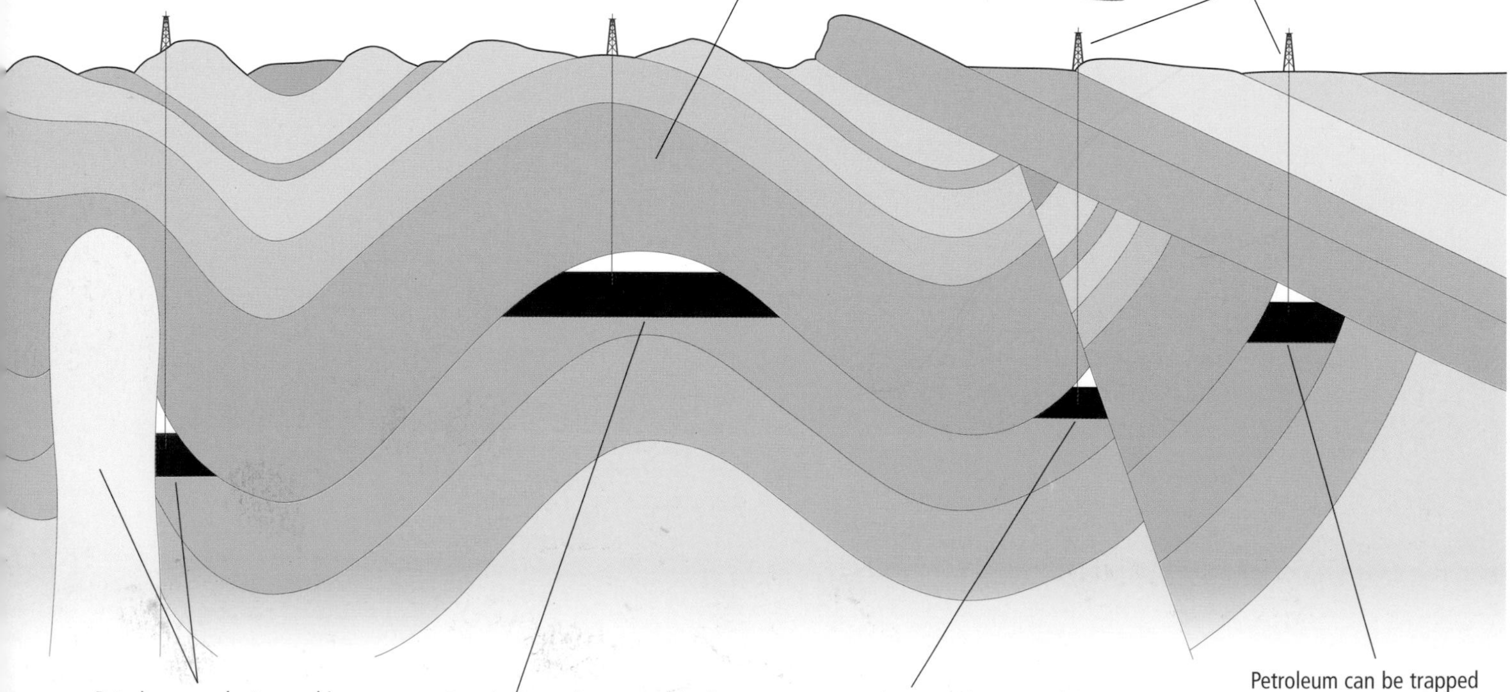

pH

A measurement of acidity. On the pH scale each number lower down indicates a tenfold increase in acidity. Neutral on the scale is 7. Numbers larger than 7 are alkaline, and values less than 7 are acid. Normal **soils** range from pH 4 to pH 8.

Phenocryst

An especially large **crystal** embedded in smaller **mineral grains**.

Placer deposit

A **sediment** containing heavy **metal grains** (for example, **gold**) that have **weathered** out of nearby **rocks** and are concentrated in a stream bed or along a coast. Gold and tin are two elements commonly recovered from placer deposits. Most historic gold rushes were based on placer deposits rather than **lodes**. (*See also:* **Diamond**.)

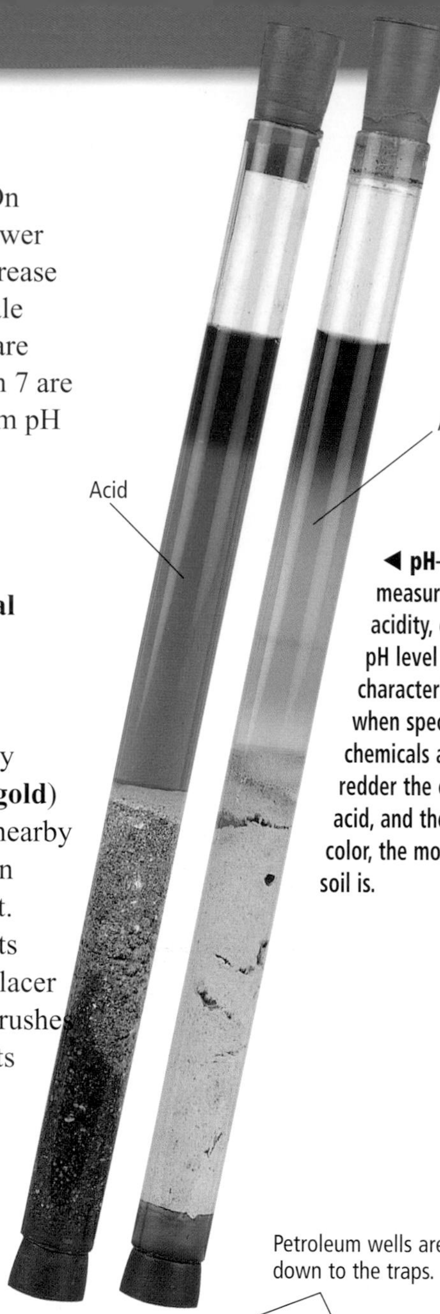

Acid

Alkaline

◄ **pH**—Soils are measured by their acidity, or pH. Each pH level produces a characteristic color when special indicating chemicals are added. The redder the color, the more acid, and the greener the color, the more alkaline a soil is.

A cap rock is impermeable to oil or natural gas.

Petroleum wells are drilled down to the traps.

Petroleum can be trapped in rocks pushed up by a salt dome.

Petroleum can be trapped in the top of an anticline or dome.

Petroleum can be trapped in a permeable rock against a fault.

Petroleum can be trapped in a permeable rock against an unconformity.

Plagioclase

The form of **feldspar** that is often white or gray. It contains sodium and calcium rather than the potassium of **orthoclase feldspar**.

Plate

(*See:* **Tectonic plate**.)

Plutonic rock

An **igneous rock** that has solidified at great depth and contains large **crystals** due to the slowness of cooling. **Intrusive rocks** may cool quickly if they are thin sheets of **magma** squeezed between cold **rock**. **Diorite** is an example of this kind of rock. But large masses of magma—for example, the magma plumes that are the sources of volcanoes—cool very slowly, giving time for many varieties of crystal to grow at the same time.

All igneous rocks formed deep underground are called plutonic rocks (after Pluto, the Greek god of the underworld). **Granites** and **gabbros** are examples of plutonic rocks. Usually, crystals in plutonic rocks are large enough to be seen with the naked eye. The texture is, therefore, **coarse**, but the **grains** are of similar size.

Podzol

An **acid soil** found in high altitudes and northerly latitudes. The surface **organic matter** decomposes slowly and releases acids that seep into the **topsoil** and **leach** the **nutrients** and iron **oxide** into the **subsoil**. This leaves a pale-colored topsoil consisting of **sand grains**.

In the subsoil iron leached from the topsoil is redeposited, staining the subsoil bright orange. Sometimes the iron is also redeposited in the form of a narrow **iron pan**.

Podzols are infertile and uncultivated. (*See also:* **Mor**.)

▶ **Podzol**—Podzol soils are very acid and show clear signs of iron movement. In both of these soil profiles the surface layer (A horizon) is black because it contains only slowly decomposing organic matter. Water interacts with the humus to produce an acid that then reacts with the soil and carries the iron away, leaving the upper soil gray. The iron is deposited lower down the profile, giving a bright orange band. This is the B horizon. The gray layer is part of the A horizon, but is often given a special letter, E, when it has lost its iron color.

Pores

The cavities between **soil** particles that are occupied by air and water. Large pores (as found in **sandy** soils) may allow too much water to be drained away, leaving the soils dry and plants subject to drought. Small pores (as found in **clay** soils) may hold the water so well that the soil becomes **waterlogged**, and air cannot get to the roots of the plants.

Loam soils are thought to have the best size of pores for allowing good drainage, yet retaining enough water for plants to use through a dry spell.

Porous

A **rock** or **soil** containing small cavities, or **pores**. Porous is not the same as **permeable**. To be permeable, the pores in a rock must connect to allow a liquid to pass through.

Porphyry, porphyritic rock

An **igneous rock** in which larger **crystals** (**phenocrysts**) are enclosed in a **fine-grained** matrix.

Prairie soil

Another word for **chernozem**.

Prismatic

A **crystal** that has formed with one **axis** very much longer than the others (*see:* **Axis of symmetry**).

Pyrite

Iron **sulfide**. Also known as "fool's gold" because of its superficial resemblance to **gold**. It is common in **sedimentary rocks** that were poor in oxygen during their formation. It sometimes fills the spaces left by ancient animals and can show the animal's shape in beautiful detail. Iron pyrite also forms yellow **cubic crystals**.

▲ **Pyrite**—Pyrite often forms cubic crystals.

Q

Quartz

A glassy **mineral** composed of silicon dioxide. Quartz is colorless when pure, but impurities can give it a variety of colors, especially brown. Quartz almost always forms irregular **grains**,

◄ **Quartz**—Quartz crystals often have a glassy appearance, as here in the case of rose quartz.

rather than **crystals**, with well-defined faces because it has a low melting point temperature and so is the last mineral to crystallize in an **igneous rock**. It fills all the remaining gaps between the crystals that have already formed. Quartz is quite hard (7 on **Mohs' scale of hardness**), and its compact structure makes it extremely resistant to **weathering**. As a result, it is found in igneous, **metamorphic**, and **sedimentary rocks**. Quartz is the most common mineral in **sandstone**, where it makes up most of the **sand** grains.

R

Regional metamorphism

Changes in **rocks** resulting from both heat and pressure. It is usually connected with mountain building and occurs over a large area. The main rocks formed by regional metamorphism are **schists** and **gneisses**. (*See also:* **Contact metamorphism** and **Metamorphic rock**.)

Rendzina

A thin **soil** that develops directly on **limestone** or **chalk rock**. The soil consists of a thin, dark **topsoil** in which there is a large percentage of **organic matter**. There is no **subsoil**. The topsoil rests directly on the rock. (*See also:* **Alkaline soil**.)

Reniform

Kidney-shaped (for example, **hematite**).

Reservoir rock

A **permeable rock** in which **petroleum** accumulates. It is overlain by a **cap rock** that prevents the petroleum from rising further.

Reversed fault

A **fault** where one slab of the Earth's **crust** rides up over another. Reversed faults are only common during **tectonic plate** collision. (*See also:* **Normal fault**.)

Rhyolite

An acidic **lava** whose **mineral** content is similar to **granite**. It is a very sticky lava, associated with explosive eruptions. It does not flow broadly and quickly solidifies, often before extensive **crystals** can form. It has a number of glassy variants that emerge on the surface, including **obsidian** and pumice. Rhyolite may show flow banding and may even have some visible crystals in it.

Pumice is often formed at the surface of rhyolitic lava, as gases try to escape, but become trapped by the stickiness of the lava. The large number of cavities in pumice gives it the appearance of a brittle, gray-colored sponge.

Rill

A small channel formed in **soil** by running water. It is small enough to be plowed out. If allowed to grow, a rill will develop into a gully (*see:* **Gulleying**).

Rock

A naturally occurring solid material containing one or more **minerals**.

(*For the main rock types see:* **Acid rock; Agglomerate; Alkaline rock; Arenaceous; Argillaceous; Arkose; Basic rock; Breccia; Calcareous rock; Chemical rock; Clastic rock; Coarse-grained rocks; Conglomerate; Extrusive rock; Fine-grained rocks; Igneous rock; Impermeable; Intrusive rock; Layered rock; Metamorphic rock; Ore; Permeable rock; Plutonic rock; Porphyritic rock; Sedimentary rock**.)

▶ **Rock**—Limestone, a sedimentary rock.

◀ **Rock**—Gabbro, an igneous rock.

▶ **Rock**—Marble, a metamorphic rock.

◀ **Rhyolite**—Rhyolite often develops a frothy surface material called pumice. It is gray.

Rock cycle

The continuous sequence of events that causes mountains to be formed, then **eroded**, before being formed again.

▼ **Rock cycle**—The diagram shows how rocks can be eroded and redeposited where they form as layers and eventually make new rocks. These rocks may then be uplifted to make new mountains.

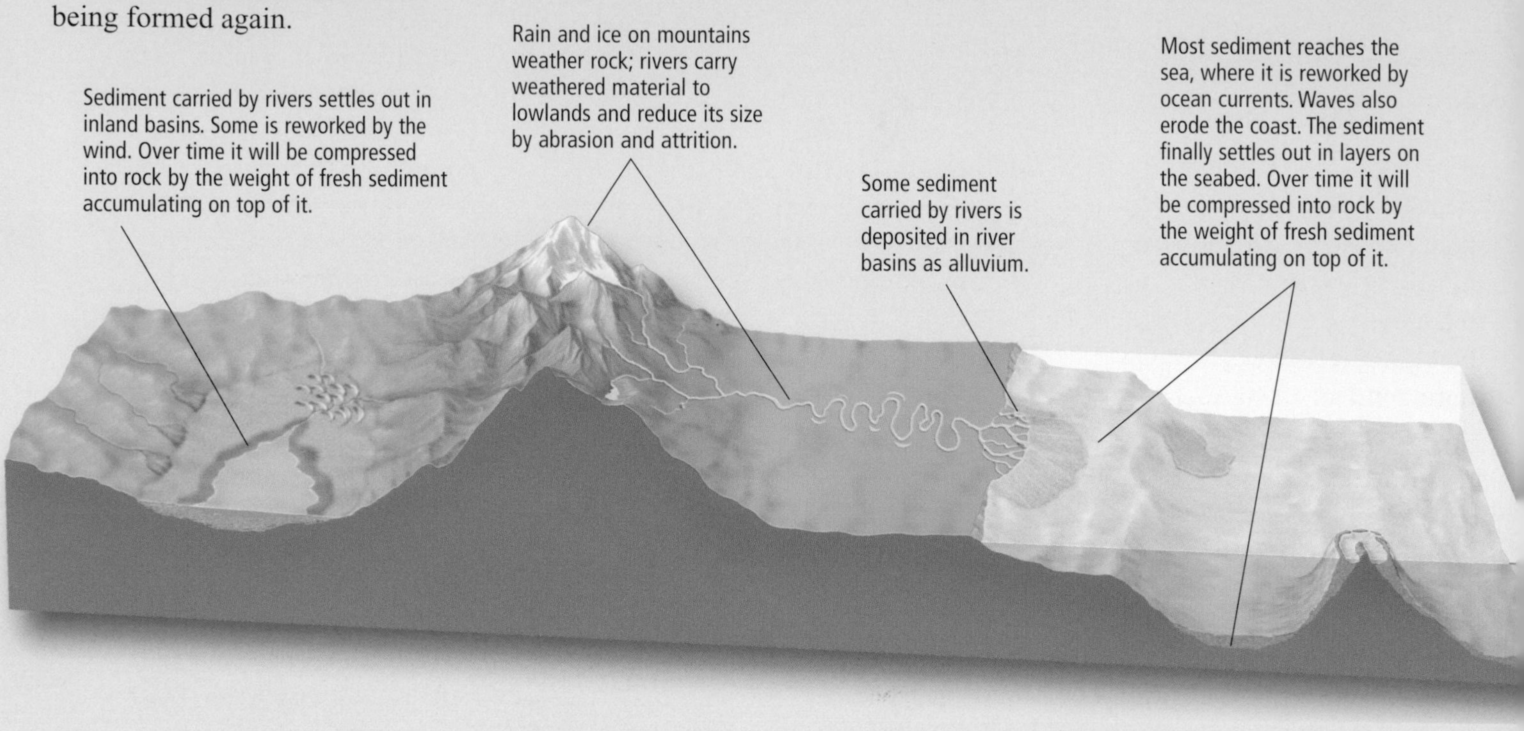

Sediment carried by rivers settles out in inland basins. Some is reworked by the wind. Over time it will be compressed into rock by the weight of fresh sediment accumulating on top of it.

Rain and ice on mountains weather rock; rivers carry weathered material to lowlands and reduce its size by abrasion and attrition.

Some sediment carried by rivers is deposited in river basins as alluvium.

Most sediment reaches the sea, where it is reworked by ocean currents. Waves also erode the coast. The sediment finally settles out in layers on the seabed. Over time it will be compressed into rock by the weight of fresh sediment accumulating on top of it.

Rock-forming minerals

Although the chemical elements occur in many thousands of **minerals**, just a few minerals are common in **rocks**. They are called the rock-forming minerals.

It is important to know about the minerals that form rocks because their hardness, solubility, and other properties can help explain why the rock is hard or soft, and how it was formed. The main rock-forming minerals are **feldspars**, **micas**, **quartz**, **ferromagnesian minerals**, **clay minerals**, **evaporite** minerals, **calcite**, and **dolomite**.

S

Salinization

The buildup of salt on or near the surface of a **soil**. It happens in deserts or near desert areas where soils are not properly irrigated. The **irrigation** water (which contains dissolved **minerals**, including salt) does not drain through the soil, but is pulled back to the surface as the soil dries out.

The process may be accelerated where irrigation water is pumped from an underground supply such as an **aquifer** that contains a very high dissolved mineral content. When this water evaporates, the minerals are left as deposits in the soil **pores** or as a crust on the surface.

Salt dome

A balloon-shaped mass of salt produced by salt being forced upward under pressure. When salt **beds** are put under pressure, they behave like liquids. If there is a weakness in an overlying **rock**, the salt will bulge up through the weakness to form a plug or dome-shaped body of salt.

Sand

Particles of **rocks** with a size between 0.06mm and 2mm. The basis of **sandstone rock**. (*See also:* **Grain**; **Grit**; **Silt**.)

▶ **Sandstone**—Sandstones are made of sand grains cemented together. The dark band in this sandstone is cemented with iron oxide. The lighter bands are cemented with calcite.

Sandstone

A **sedimentary rock** composed of cemented **sand**-sized **grains** 0.06mm and 2mm in diameter. The nature of the cement affects the hardness and color of the sandstone. If the cement is **calcite**, the sandstone is a pale color and not particularly resistant to **chemical weathering**. If the cement is iron **oxide**, the sandstone

Sandy soil

A **soil** in which there is enough sand to keep the **clay** particles from clumping together and forming a **crumb structure**. Sandy soils are easily **eroded** because they do not have a good **soil structure**.

Schist

A **metamorphic rock** that can be identified by its shiny surface of **mica crystals** all pointing in the same direction. It is formed by high pressure and temperature during mountain building. (*See also:* **Foliation**.)

Scoria

The rough, often foamlike **rock** that forms on the surface of some **lavas**.

Sediment

Any layer of particles that have settled from moving water or wind.

The sea is the final resting place for most of the material **eroded** from the land. So, **layered rocks** are mainly formed in the still waters of the sea.

Each layer of rock represents a time when a particular kind of material was laid down. A deposit of **sand** may be compressed to make **sandstone**, mud may be compressed to make **shale**, and so on.

Each kind of sediment gives a clue to the conditions that occurred when the sediment was laid down. Sediments that are coarse, like sand, can only be carried by swift currents. Fine sediments like mud can only settle where the water is still. Rivers, for example, have lots of energy to keep material on the move while they are in a channel. But when the material reaches the still water of the open sea, the material will settle out on the seabed.

Where the material settles out depends on how big it is. If the material is the size of a pebble or a **grain** of sand when it reaches the sea, it will be deposited near the coast. In time pebbles will form a rock called **conglomerate**; sand will form sandstone. Mud, on the other hand, will remain suspended in the water until it is far away from the coastal currents. Only then will it settle out and perhaps become compressed into shale. (*See also:* **Facies** and **Formation**.)

Sediment deposited by a river is called alluvium (*see:* **Alluvial soil**). Sediments from wind-blown materials indicate where sand dunes once formed. They often make thick **beds**. (*See also:* **Bedding plane**; **Cross-bedding**; **Current bedding**; **Facies**; **Geosyncline**; **Placer deposit**; **Sedimentary rock**.)

Sedimentary rock

A **rock** formed as pieces of **mineral**, rock, animal, or vegetable matter settled from flowing water or wind.

The main sedimentary rocks are **shales** (from **clay**) and **sandstone** (from **sand**). Some **limestones** also form as sedimentary rocks. Siltstones and **conglomerates** are less common sedimentary rocks.

Some sedimentary rocks, such as **graywackes**, show no layering. (*See also:* **Cross-bedding**; **Facies**; **Layered rock**; **Sediment**; **Stratum**; **Unconformity**.)

▶ Sandstone— This butte is made of many beds of sandstone.

is red from the iron and resistant to chemical weathering. If the cement is **silica**, the **rock** is pale in color but extremely resistant to chemical weathering. (*See also:* **Arenaceous**; **Acid soil**; **Arkose**; **Clastic rock**; **Layered rock**.)

Series

The **rock** layers that correspond to an **epoch** of time.

Shale

A **fine-grained sedimentary rock** made of **clay minerals** with particle sizes smaller than 2 millionths of a meter across. It is formed from mud that built up in calm conditions on an ocean or lake bed.

(*See also:* **Argillaceous**.)

Silica, silicate

The **mineral** silicon dioxide. It is very common, occurring as, for example, **quartz**. A silicate is any mineral that contains silica.

(*For examples of silicates see:* **Augite**; **Bauxite**; **Feldspar**; **Hornblende**; **Micas**; **Olivine**.)

▼ **Shale**—Bands of rain-eroded shale in Petrified Forest National Park, Arizona.

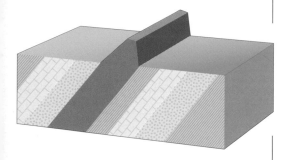

▲ **Sill**—A sill is an igneous rock that forms between other beds of rock.

Sill

A sheetlike body of **intrusive igneous rock** that has been injected between layers of **sedimentary** or **metamorphic rock**. Sills are often composed of **basalt**. (*See also:* **Contact metamorphism**.)

Silt

Particles of **rock** between 0.06mm and 0.0002mm across. Less common than **sand** or **clay**. Silt particles give a soil a soapy feel (*see:* **Silty soil**). (*See also:* **Grain** and **Grit**.)

Silty soil

A **soil** in which there is enough **silt** for it to feel soapy to the touch. Silty soils are common in places where wind-blown material called **loess** occurs. It is found in large areas of China, in parts of the prairies, and in northern Europe and Australia. Silty soils are easily **eroded** by the wind and rain if exposed, such as when the land is plowed for growing crops. Parts of the Dust Bowl region of the midwestern United States have silty soils. Huge problems of erosion face the people of China.

Silver

A silvery white, relatively soft, shiny **metal**. It has been sought after since the earliest times and is regarded as a precious metal, just as **gems** are precious stones. Silver is often found in **veins** that were once close to **magma** chambers, alongside **gold** and **copper**.

▶ **Silver**—This is native silver.

Skarn

A **mineral** deposit formed by the chemical reaction of hot, acidic fluids and **carbonate** rocks.

Slag

The rocklike material that becomes separated from **metal** during the smelting of an **ore**.

Slate

A **metamorphic rock** produced only by pressure. The **clay minerals** become arranged parallel to one another. This is the reason slate is so easy to split into sheets and use for roofing. (*See also:* **Slaty cleavage**.)

Slaty cleavage

A characteristic pattern found in **slates** in which the parallel arrangement of **clay minerals** causes the **rock** to **fracture** (cleave) in sheets.

Soil erosion

The accelerated movement of **soil** away from a field by wind or heavy rain. Soil erosion is usually a man-made problem caused by poor farming methods, especially by leaving the soil uncovered between harvesting and the growth of a new crop. (*See also:* **Erode, erosion** and **Gulleying.**)

Soil

A mixture of **mineral** and **organic matter** that forms on the surface of most **rocks**. It is the medium in which plants grow.

Soils are divided up into major soil groups based on the processes at work inside the soil.

Major soil groups each have a characteristic pattern of layers, or soil **horizons**. Common soils include **podzols**, **brown soils**, and **chernozems**.

(*See also:* **A horizon; B horizon; C horizon; Color; Conservation; Creep; Moisture; Soil erosion; Structure; Subsoil; Texture; Topsoil.**)

(*For other soil types see:* **Acid brown soil; Acid soil; Alfisol; Alkaline soil; Alluvial soil; Black soil; Calcareous soil; Chestnut soil; Desert soil; Fertile soil; Friable; Gley; Gray-brown soil; Heavy soil; Iron pan; Impermeable; Latosol; Light soil; Loam; Mountain soil; Permeable soil; Prairie soil; Rendzina; Tundra soil; Vertisol.**)

▼ **Soil**—The diagram shows how a soil might develop from a parent material. The soil forms from the surface down and is the result of chemical reactions between the water seeping downward and the minerals of the rock from which the soil is forming.

Soils have layers, or horizons. To be called a soil, the upper horizon must have organic matter in it.

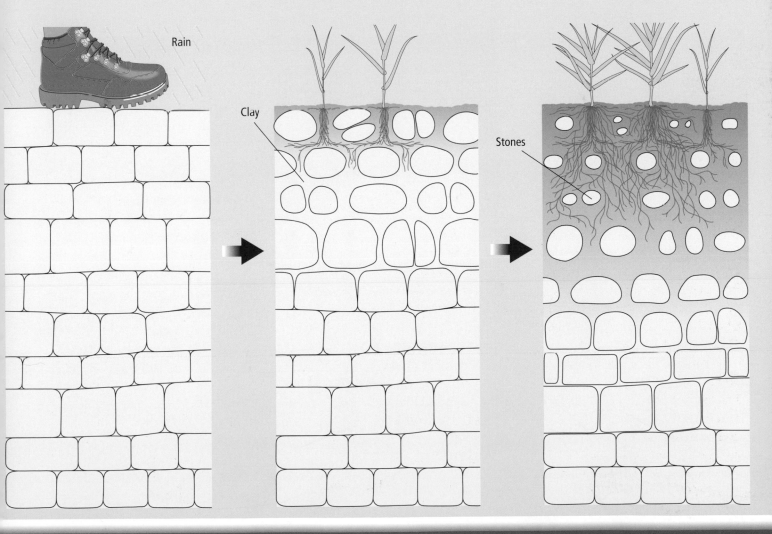

Rain

Clay

Stones

Sphalerite

A colorless **mineral** also called zinc sulfide. Any colors in it are caused by iron impurities; with increasing iron the colors change to green, brown, red, and black. Red to yellow sphalerite does not look like a **metal**, being **transparent** or **translucent** and looking something like dull amber. Black sphalerite looks more metallic. Sphalerite containing cadmium is bright orange.

Zinc sulfide is the most abundant and important zinc mineral. It is also called zinc blende. Sphalerite comes from the Greek *sphaleros*, meaning treacherous.

▶ **Sphalerite**—The crystals of sphalerite are the darker ones. Intermixed with them are pyrite (yellow) and calcite (transparent).

Stalactites and stalagmites

A stalactite is a rocklike column that hangs from the roof of a cave. A stalagmite is a similar feature that grows up from the floor of a cave.

Both are the result of carbonate-rich water flowing through **limestone**. When the carbonate-rich water reaches a cave, some of the carbonate comes out of solution and becomes rock once more.

This happens especially at places where water drips from cave roofs, or where it splashes onto cave floors. Over thousands of years tiny amounts of precipitated calcium carbonate (**calcite**) build up into spectacular features, sometimes tens of meters long.

▼ **Stalactites and stalagmites**—These are needlelike deposits of calcite that mostly form within caves.

Stock

A vertical protrusion of a **batholith** that pushes up closer to the surface.

Stratigraphy

The study of the Earth's **rocks** to try to find out their history and conditions under which they formed.

Stratovolcano

A volcano of the common cone type. The cone is formed by layers of **ash** and **lava** built up over time and as the result of many eruptions.

Stratum, strata

A layer or layers of **sedimentary rock**.

Streak

The colored line produced by rubbing a **mineral** against a piece of unglazed white porcelain. This is used as a test when identifying minerals.

Structure, soil

The way **soil** particles are held together. Soil particles are held together in clumps by **humus** and by calcium in the soil. If the soil has enough of both of them, it will usually form into small ball-shaped clumps. This is called a **crumb structure**. It is most commonly found in the **topsoil**.

In the **subsoil** there is little humus, and so a crumb structure does not form. Subsoils in **sandy** materials do not form any kind of structure. Subsoils in **clay** materials are affected by shrinking and swelling as they dry out and become wet from season to season. This tends to break the soil into blocks and produce a blocky structure.

Structure is important because plant roots need good drainage and aeration. Crumb and blocky structures help provide this.

Subsoil

Also known as the **B horizon**, the subsoil is the part of the **soil** below the **topsoil** (**A horizon**) and above the **parent material** (**C horizon**). The subsoil is the thickest part of the soil. It contains very little **organic matter**. Roots in the subsoil do not find nourishment, but only water. Some plants have hardly any roots in the subsoil.

Sulfides

A group of important **ore minerals** (for example, **pyrite**, **galena**, and **sphalerite**) in which **sulfur** combines with one or more **metals**.

Sulfur

An element and a **mineral** that can occur on its own as bright yellow and amber **crystals**, and in combination with many **metals**, for example, as iron **pyrites**, iron sulfide. The element can form crystals in more than one **crystal system**.

   Most sulfur becomes deposited directly from volcanic gases and so commonly occurs in volcanic rocks (*see:* **Igneous rock**).

Superficial deposit

Any layer of material that has been laid down over solid **rocks**. It may be used to describe alluvium or **loess**. This material is often many meters thick. The term is not used to describe soils.

T

Talc

A common gray-brown **mineral** in **metamorphic rocks**. Another word for talc is soapstone. The word talc comes from the Arabic *talq*, meaning "mica."

▲ **Sulfur**—Sulfur often forms bright yellow crystals near volcanoes and geysers.

Tectonic plate

A large piece of the solid, brittle outer part of the Earth that moves over the surface of the Earth independently of other parts of the **crust**.

▼ **Tectonic plate**—Tectonic plates, or just "plates," are most significant where they push together to form new mountains. These are places where metamorphic rocks are made. New volcanic materials rise to the surface from both colliding plates and where plates pull apart.

Texture, soil

The proportion of **sand**, **silt**, and **clay** particles in a **soil**. If a soil has more sand than clay or silt, it has a sandy texture. When clay dominates, a soil has a clayey texture; and when silt is the most common size of particles, the soil has a silty texture. Roughly equal proportions of all sizes of particle are called a **loam**.

   Sandy-textured soils warm up quickly in spring and drain well in winter but may be prone to dry out in summer. Clay soils warm up slowly in spring and may **waterlog** in winter. If they dry out in summer, they may crack open.

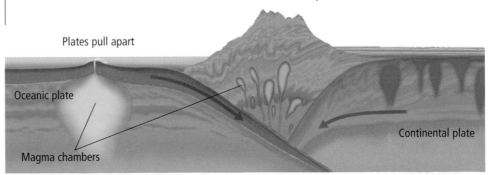

New mountains form where plates collide.

Plates pull apart

Oceanic plate

Magma chambers

Continental plate

Topsoil

A surface layer (or **A horizon**) of a **soil**. This **horizon** is vital for plant growth because it contains most of the **nutrients** that plants needs. A dark, deep topsoil provides the best conditions for plant growth.

Translucent

A **mineral** that allows light to penetrate but not pass through it. (*See also:* **Gypsum**.)

Transparent

A **mineral** that allows light to pass right through it.

Triclinic

A **crystal system** in which none of the three axes in a crystal is at right angles or of equal length to one another (*see:* **Axis of symmetry**).

Tuff

A **rock** made of volcanic **ash**. Volcanic activity produces a large amount of ash that settles over the landscape. It is particularly thick close to the vent of a volcano. After an eruption has ended, the ash begins to consolidate, and a later covering with **lava** or more ash will turn the ash into a soft rock. This is tuff. In effect, the rock could be thought of as a **sediment** because it has been laid down from the air, but the material is entirely **igneous**, and it forms only at the time of an eruption. (*See also:* **Agglomerate**.)

Tundra soil

Soils that form in the cold, wet conditions of the northernmost latitudes. They are typically **waterlogged** and have a thin, black **mor** surface **horizon**. In this horizon rainwater becomes acidic; when it washes down into the rest of the **topsoil**, it carries away **nutrients**. Most tundra soils show little development of topsoil and **subsoil** because they are frozen for most of the year.

U

Unconformity

Any interruption in the way that **sedimentary rocks** are laid down. It is usually marked by a change in the kind of **sediment**, for example, a change from red **sandstones** formed in a desert to **shales** formed under a sea. The discovery of unconformities was one of the landmark steps on the way to explaining Earth history. Before this discovery it was thought that all rocks were laid down at the same time by a single great flood.

Unconsolidated

▲ **Unconformity**—Unconformities are most striking at junctions where rocks lie with different angles to their beds.

▶ **Vein**—Bands of minerals passing across a rock.

deposit

Any layer of material that has been laid down over solid **rocks**. It may be used to describe deposits from an ice sheet, alluvium, coastal **sand**, or **loess**. This material is often many meters thick. The term is not used to describe **soils**.

V

Vein

A sheetlike body made only of **minerals** (for example, **quartz**) that cuts across a **rock**. Veins are often important sources of minerals. Miners also call such important veins **lodes**. (*See also:* **Contact metamorphism** and **Gangue**.)

Vertisol

A **clay**-rich **soil** of the subtropics that is dominated by swelling clays. During the wet season the soil swells as the clays take up water and expand. In the dry season the clays dry out, and the soil cracks badly.

The swelling and shrinking are so severe that they continually churn over the soil, making it very difficult to use for farming. These soils are, however, very **fertile** and can be used for crops, provided **irrigation** is applied in such a way that the **moisture** content of the soils is kept constant throughout the year. (*See also:* **Black soil**.)

Vesicle

A small cavity in a volcanic **rock** originally created by an air bubble trapped in the molten **lava**. (*See also:* **Amygdule** and **Basalt**.)

Viscous, viscosity

Words that describe the ease with which a liquid flows. If a liquid flows slowly, the liquid is said to be very viscous. **Lavas**, for example can be runny (and have a low viscosity), or they can be sticky (and have a high viscosity).

Volcanic rock

(*See:* **Igneous rock**.)

W

Waterlog, waterlogged soil

A **soil** that holds rainwater, causing it to pond up at the surface.

Soils become waterlogged for two reasons. First, because the soils form on a flood plain with water close to the surface. They become waterlogged when the water table rises during the winter. This kind of soil is waterlogged in the **subsoil**. If this happens for a large part of the year, the subsoil turns gray. Second, soils become waterlogged if they are dominated by **clays**. A clay soil has only very small soil **pores**, and water cannot get through them. As a result the

soil becomes waterlogged at the surface, and if this is prolonged, the **topsoil** turns gray, and **peat** forms on the surface. (*See also:* **Gley**.)

Weathering, weather

The process of breaking down a **rock** into smaller pieces. There are two kinds of weathering.

First, weathering may happen because of changes in temperature, particularly when water freezes. Any water trapped in cracks in a rock will expand as it freezes. The force involved can easily be enough

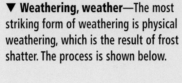

▼ **Weathering, weather**—The most striking form of weathering is physical weathering, which is the result of frost shatter. The process is shown below.

to break up rock. This kind of weathering produces large, sharp-edged pieces, or flakes. This is called physical weathering and is shown in the diagram below.

Second, weathering can occur because of rainfall. This is called **chemical weathering**. Rain is slightly acidic and will react with rock, causing new substances to be formed. The main substance formed is **clay**.

All the products of rainfall (chemical) weathering are too small to be seen except with the most powerful microscopes.

Rainfall (chemical) weathering produces soils worldwide.

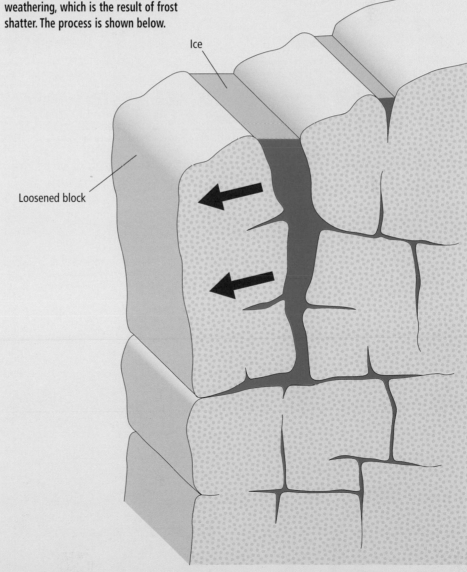

Ice

Loosened block

Index